The Middle of Things

The Middle of Things

— *Essays* —

By
Meghan Florian

CASCADE *Books* • Eugene, Oregon

THE MIDDLE OF THINGS
Essays

Cascade Books
An Imprint of Wipf and Stock Publishers
199 W. 8th Ave., Suite 3
Eugene, OR 97401

www.wipfandstock.com

PAPERBACK ISBN: 978-1-5326-0715-8
HARDCOVER ISBN: 978-1-5326-0717-2
EBOOK ISBN: 978-1-5326-0716-5

Cataloguing-in-Publication data:

Names: Florian, Meghan.

Title: The middle of things : essays / Meghan Florian.

Description: Eugene, OR: Cascade Books, 2017 | Includes bibliographical references and index.

Identifiers: ISBN 978-1-5326-0715-8 (paperback) | ISBN 978-1-5326-0717-2 (hardcover) | ISBN 978-1-5326-0716-5 (ebook)

Subjects: LCSH: Florian, Meghan | Memoir | Kirkegaard, Søren

Classification: B4376 .F56 2017 (paperback) | CALL NUMBER (ebook)

Manufactured in the U.S.A.   06/23/17

For Laura

Contents

Acknowledgments

For their unfailing belief in my work and my words, I am grateful to and for . . .

My family: Mom, Dad, Holly, Andrew, Heidi, and Eric; Laura, my best friend and ideal reader; Ruthan, Katherine, Kara, and Amy; my professors, especially Jim Allis and Jack Mulder; Gordon Marino and the Kierkegaard Library at St. Olaf College; The Collegeville Institute; my Queens MFA family, especially Alpha Krappy Grammar, Suzannah Lessard, Michael Kobre, and Fred Leebron; *Lunch Ticket*, *Rhubarb*, and *Windhover*, where earlier versions of several of these essays appeared; Chapel Hill Mennonite Fellowship; Fullsteam Brewery; and finally, The Shadowboxers, though they may never read this, because if they hadn't had that sound check party in Minneapolis, I might never have figured out how to begin.

Camp Kierkegaard

———

Sandheden er en Snare: Du kan ikke faae den, uden at Du fanges;
Du kan ikke faae Sandheden saaledes at Du fanger den, men kun
saaledes, at den fanger Dig.

The Truth is a snare: you cannot get it without being caught yourself; you cannot get the truth by catching it yourself but only by
its catching you.

—Søren Kierkegaard[1]

For the third summer in four years, I returned to Northfield,
Minnesota for two precious weeks of writing and research at
St. Olaf College's Kierkegaard Library. This would be my summer
vacation. Granted that a vacation spent studying philosophy may
sound unappealing to most, the quiet and focus of a small college
town in summer was all I wanted as an escape from the other em-
ployment that takes me away from my own research for much of
the school year. A small town with few distractions outside of the
local pub is as nice a place as any I can imagine for such a retreat.

Still, while I was there, an up-and-coming band I had been
following for a few years was playing a show in Minneapolis, and
this seemed like an appropriate opportunity to get out of my head
for a while, have a few drinks, and dance—to remind myself I am

1. Kierkegaard, *Journalen* NB31.37 SKS 26,21.

not a word-producing machine, and that vacations are meant to be fun. I'd written 5,000-plus words in my first week at the library, on top of daily marathon reading sessions. I was due for some kind of break.

I was still hemming and hawing about whether it was worth the hour and a half bus trip each way from tiny Northfield to the city, though, which would cost more than the concert ticket itself, when I got an email from the band's tour manager informing me I'd won a spot—for myself and a friend—at the band's sound check party the next day.

I emailed her back and said it would be just me. I laid aside my copy of *The Two Ages* and bought my bus ticket. Then my social anxiety kicked in.

I go to concerts alone all the time, but hanging out *with the band*? A test of my self-confidence. I texted my best friend, joking about the likelihood of making a fool of myself, and began to stress out about what to wear in order to look less like a nutty professor. (Black skinny jeans, chambray shirt, Birkenstocks—was I trendy or nerdy, with my tortoise shell Warby Parker frames? Is nerdy-chic a thing, I wondered, and if so, can I pull it off?) Lamenting the limited options in my suitcase, I nevertheless got dressed on Friday and headed into the city. Nerves would not stop me. I really liked their music. And they were cute. If I fell on my face in front of them, I would at least get a good story out of it.

I got to the venue early and milled about awkwardly by the sign where Ginelle, the tour manager, told me to meet her. I considered smoking one of the clove cigarettes in my purse, a vice I embrace on research trips, though never at home, but thought better of it, not wanting my first impression to be wreathed in smoke, even if it would add to the aura of mysterious existentialist I seem to cultivate in spite of myself. Eventually two other women joined me—*young* women, maybe twenty-two, in high heels and thick make-up that immediately made me want to sink into the side-walk. I tried to breathe in calm and breathe out cool, as Ginelle walked us in, down the steps to the basement venue. I blinked as my eyes adjusted, tried to make confident eye contact with the band, on stage, where they'd already started warming up.

I'm the Cool Girl, I thought. Though normally I hate the concept, and all such reductive categorizing of women, I tried to believe it was true. It's easy to feel cool when surrounded by philosophers, at least some of whom have earned the stereotypes we press upon them. Lots of tweed, elbow patches, receding hairlines, and few small talk skills. The "real" world where I was spending this weekend cast that world in sharp relief.

The other women introduced themselves. I could sense them moving toward a metaphorical center stage in our impromptu trio of fangirls. In the dwindling days of my thirtieth year, I was aware that the confident cool that took most of my twenties to develop was now already fading into the shadows cast by other, younger women. In ordinary life, I am less Cool Girl or even Smart Girl than I am Invisible Woman. I am no longer simply uncool; now I am *aging*. If you were never the hot one to begin with, wrinkles certainly aren't going to improve matters.

Did I mention these musicians were cute?

I rocked back and forth in my Birkenstocks, smiling shyly. I love this band's music, and I'm not one to base my fandom on physical attractiveness, but I'm not *blind*. Or maybe it's just that anyone who can harmonize like these guys is attractive to me, regardless of aesthetic realities. Maybe they're not even that cute, rather their voices had addled my brain. Perhaps it's just that inexplicable quality Kierkegaard's Young Man drones on about in "In Vino Veritas"—"if love is ludicrous, it is just as ludicrous whether I find a princess or a servant girl," he says.[2] In my case, one might paraphrase: a crush is just as ludicrous whether he be a musician or a philosopher.

All of this only served to make me nervous, now that I was in the same room with them, now that they were taking song requests, from *me* (and the pretty young things in their tall shoes).

We sat on stools in the back as they played, and I loosened up. They were funny, the guys in the band. Normal guys, not rock

2. Kierkegaard, *Stages on Life's Way*, 37.

stars—the kind of guys I might have hung out with in college, I thought. College—longer ago for me than for them. They bantered from the stage, and their banter had a relaxing effect on me, my stress releasing with each laugh.

They finished the sound check, though, and I remembered that I was still a thirty-year-old introverted philosopher in Birkenstocks. Thirty. So young in the grand scheme of years, yet perhaps too old to be a fangirl, I realized belatedly.

We milled about. The band guys introduced themselves, asked how I came to listen to their music. I softened as I told them about seeing them open for the Indigo Girls in Raleigh a few years ago. We talked about Amy Ray. They expressed confusion about why I was in Minneapolis when I am living in Durham, and I offered a suitably vague answer. They told a story about the time they played at Motorco, a venue near me in Durham, and I felt retroactive sadness that I missed it.

I sat on a stool, and one of the guitarists, Scott, sat down next to me. Scott, I had decided, is the cutest one.

He introduced himself, and we made conversation the way you would if you met someone somewhere ordinary, not at a private party before his band's show in a tiny venue in the Midwest, not as a fangirl and a guitarist. I felt better, talking to him. I felt glad that I came, though now I was focused on how easily I lost track of what he was saying because of the light in his dark eyes, looking at *me*. He glanced around, apologized, said he just wanted to be sure there wasn't something else he should be doing—it's the first time they've done one of these things.

I took him to mean he wasn't sure it was okay that he was talking only to me, and I smiled my shy smile again. He asked me why I was in Minnesota, and this time I didn't give the vague answer. I blame his eyes for magicking the truth out of me. Eye contact, the source of so much accidental truth telling.

"I'm doing research at the Kierkegaard Library at St. Olaf College," I told him. "It's like philosophy camp for grown-ups."

Away flew any chance I had of pulling off the Cool Girl act.

He laughed, this delightful laugh. "That is the nerdiest thing I have ever heard . . . I love it." He smiled, his eyes dropping for a moment as his body moved with laughter. And then he said this: "I studied philosophy in college."

DANGER. Cute musician also likes philosophy. No good can come of this.

"But I've never read any Kierkegaard. What's his thing?"

I am sorry to say I gave a terrible introduction to Kierkegaard—I rambled about Abraham, about the Knight of Faith, which isn't even my favorite part of Kierkegaard's work. What a missed opportunity. If I were a true Kierkegaardian Flirt I would have drawn on all of my knowledge of *Works of Love* and *Stages on Life's Way* to discuss passion, preference, all the subtle nuances of self-deception and seduction in the works I've studied for nearly a decade now. Alas, the moment passed. I resolve to do better, next time.

Scott told one of the other guys the real reason I was in Minnesota, completely blowing my cover. I was back in my normal role as aging nerd, as the Smart Girl. And it was okay. A decade studying philosophy has taught me that such resistance to my deeper self is futile. Nights like this, when I fought it, are more and more rare. I've changed; I am no longer twenty-two, thank God.

The band prepared to leave for dinner. I would see them again later, for the show, though we'd be separated then by lights and a crowd. "The crowd is untruth," I think, according to Kierkegaard. But the laughter in Scott's eyes was true.

We took a picture, we said goodbye.

Scott hugged me. Those smiling eyes made contact with mine once more, and it seemed somehow that being the Smart Girl is not half bad.

Kierkegaard would have a field day with me, I'm sure.

When I began college at nineteen I had never read a single page of philosophical writing. I would have struggled to tell you what philosophy actually was if you had asked me. As a high school student I had always assumed I was going to study English in college, and be a writer. I also assumed that I would spend my life waiting tables.

Philosophy drew me in over time. One might think that the obsession with big ideas that consumed me in college was just a phase, abandoned as soon I found a slightly more realistic career path. Philosophy, after all, is the only major that gets made fun of more than English when it comes to potential for success. "Would you like fries with that?" people asked me, when I changed my major.

Yes, I would, thank you very much. Pass the ketchup.

Everything I ever liked or was good at was something that would mean struggling to support myself, and in college I worried about my future far more than was good for me. I lived in my head most of the time. I remember sitting in one of the roomy arm-chairs in the common room of my all women's dormitory at Hope College a week or two into the semester, the Norton *Anthology of Western World Literature* in my lap, reading *The Iliad,* pleased to be in a 200-level literature class with mostly sophomores during my first semester, but feeling like I may have gotten in over my head. Lindsey, who lived across the hall from me, walked in and paused outside her door.

"Meghan, you read *all the time,*" she said. I looked up, puzzled. Wasn't that what college was for? I shrugged and went back to reading at a snail's pace, hoping at some point things would start to click in my head. The literary world of the ancient Greeks fascinated me more than the conversations I overheard in the common room about boys or weekend parties (which usually drove me back into my tiny cinder block room to work). With time I became more comfortable with my ability to interpret the works I was studying; I did not understand fashion or dating, but I understood books. It helped when I got an A on my first college paper, too. I wish I could re-read that paper now, but it is lost to a world in which I still used floppy disks—bright purple ones, purchased at the college bookstore, and transported from one computer lab to the next.

Though my grades were good, I remained quiet in classes. I spent Saturdays at the library, and evenings reading in coffee shops with the studious friends I slowly unearthed. I doubted my own voice, and rarely expressed my opinions. I was not sure what my opinions were half the time. Then, toward the end of my first year of college, my advisor suggested that I take a philosophy course the following fall. It would be wise in case I ever decided to go to graduate school, she said, and besides that she thought I might enjoy it.

I laughed at the suggestion of graduate school. The thought had never even crossed my mind. I was part of the first generation in my family to attend a four-year college, and just getting this far seemed like an awful lot of education to me (and my parents). I had no idea why people went to graduate school in the first place, unless it was to become a medical doctor or a lawyer. As the sort of well-behaved young woman who takes her professors' advice, however, I registered for Intro to Philosophy.

It was an eight-week, two-credit course that changed everything. "The Body" was the focus of the class, and we read both ancient and contemporary texts. Once a week we were required to write a one-page response paper about anything that struck us in the reading assignment for the day—these were to be "shitty first drafts," Dr. Allis told us, quoting Anne Lamott, doing his best to quell our nervousness about writing philosophically. I wrote a diatribe in response to that first week's reading (I am sorry to say I cannot remember who we read) about the distinction between *having* a body, and *being* a body. Caught up in a culture of female body shaming, my response as a young woman was gnosticism—I wanted to disassociate from my body. My body was not *me*. A rose by any other name would smell as sweet, I said, and a six-foot-tall Meghan with red hair and green eyes would be no different from the five-foot-tall brunette I actually inhabited. A body was just a body.

My classmate Sarah had written something very different, and when Dr. Allis put us in discussion groups and we read our words to one another, I found myself playing intellectual ping-pong with

7

her, and questioning my own perspective. Was a body perhaps more than I was willing to let it be? Was I being just as reductive as the body-shaming culture I critiqued, reducing myself to a mind or a personality? What did it mean to be *embodied*—to experienced myself holistically? My whole understanding of personhood turned upside down.

I do not remember what other courses I took that semester. What I remember is meeting my best friend Laura for lunch after philosophy class, and talking her ear off about the material we were covering. I remember that I spoke up in class on a regular basis. I remember Dr. Allis telling me to call him Jim (though I continued to call him Dr. Allis until I was a senior). I remember that he wrote "Thank you for your work" on every single paper I wrote for him, and that I knew he meant it.

I am sure that many, many people in my life had believed in me over the years. I had always gotten good grades, been described as having "potential." But I never believed it. Who can say what was responsible for that mental block, but something in Jim's kind eyes, his earnest thanks, both written on my papers and voiced in class, got through to me. He said that we were free to change our minds about anything we said in class five minutes after we said it, and so, for the first time, I felt free to try something and get it wrong. For a lifelong perfectionist, a people-pleasing middle child, that was what I needed more than anything. Permission to fail, and begin again.

If I ever did find those purple floppy disks I am sure I would find much that would embarrass me now, but it was the process that mattered. I was learning how to think. As Kierkegaard (a philosopher I would soon encounter) put it when discussing his authorial position in *My Point of View as an Author*, I was learning "in *working* also to *work against oneself*."[3] I developed an internal dialogue, and a renewed sense of wonder and curiosity about the world around me, as I worked out my own thoughts.

My mind was set on fire. Existence, embodiment, epistemology—these words rolled around in my head, and eventually off my

3. Kierkegaard, *The Point of View*, 9.

tongue, as I learned a new language, delighting in a foreign tongue, coming to rest in a new land where I began to feel at home for the first time in my young adult life. I barely paused when considering my courses for the next semester. Modern Philosophy was the clear choice, and my advisor encouraged me to follow the rabbit trail and see where it led me.

It led me to Søren Kierkegaard.

Long before I started reading the famous Danish Lutheran philosopher, known to some as the "father of existentialism," I had begun a faith struggle of my own. Raised in the Christian Reformed Church by parents strongly influenced by Baptist and evangelical Christianity, and attending a small religious college in the west Michigan "bible belt," my life had always been influenced by the church. Even as an adolescent, though, my busy mind had wrestled with big questions. In my high school Sunday school classes, while I reveled in—and sometimes struggled with—the language of the Heidelberg Catechism, my peers seemed bored, simply accepting the faith their families had practiced for generations. While others attended football games on the weekends, I was at home poring over C. S. Lewis's *Mere Christianity*. I scribbled ordinary teen angst in my journal, yet my prose was also peppered with thoughts on the universe and God and my place in the order of things.

Now, as a college student, I was in the midst of a crisis—a *dark night of the soul*, as theological types like to call it. I was taking courses on bible and religion and philosophy that stretched the boundaries of what I thought I knew, of what I was *capable* of knowing. I hadn't given up on church, but I had a new set of questions, more skeptical than those of my C. S. Lewis days. In my Old Testament class we studied historical critical methods of interpretation, and as I learned more of the details of by whom and how the biblical canon was constructed, instead of lashing out like some of my peers did—denying this method if interpretation in favor of infallibility—I accepted it. But I didn't know what to *do* with this new knowledge. The bible had not dropped from the sky in one piece. It contained contradictions, dare I say flaws, with which I did not know how to cope.

My professor somehow still managed to believe in biblical truth, and the church, despite knowing that this primary Christian text was written by human hands, and as such contained ordinary human inconsistencies. How? Why? What did he hold on to? What motivated him to continue to read the bible as *Scripture*? And what about all the theology I was becoming interested in, which was based on biblical texts? Could I find a way to hold onto that, or should I give that up, too? I did not know how to interpret the bible anymore, and so I simply stopped reading it at all. I asked myself, maybe for the first time, whether the God I thought I believed in really—*really*—existed, and I found no answers.

Yet, despite all of this, for some unexplainable reason I decided it was a good idea to sign up for an evangelism-focused spring break "mission trip" in Los Angeles. Evangelism is exactly what a person should be doing when she's at a place in life where she wakes up every morning and wonders if everything she's built her life on is something made up by a bunch of dead guys, right?

It was as if I thought by somehow pushing myself beyond what church leaders kept calling my "comfort zone" I could, maybe, experience some kind of miracle. Perhaps God would give me some revelation, if only I showed enough faith.

This was a terrible plan. Instead of encountering truth, I came face-to-face with the faith I was basically *trying* to leave, but somehow couldn't quit. We spent the week hanging out with homeless folks in LA, offering gifts of food and clothing at times but mostly focusing on "sharing the gospel," and the guilt I felt in the face of that poverty was a result of realizing how little the Christianity I knew had to say to what was in front of me. What do you say when standing on a corner in Skid Row with a stack of evangelical tracts in your hand? How do you talk about a God you think you no longer believe in, yet somehow hope exists, in a place where God seems so clearly absent? Broken bodies, broken souls, broken social systems—everything around me was broken, and I was breaking, too.

To the extent that I could say I believed in the absurdity of the Christian story of God becoming human, and dying, and that death somehow saving humanity from some sort of hell or damnation, at the end of the day, I still asked myself the "Why?" questions. Why did I think I should be here? Why do any of us think we are supposed to help others? Why would it even occur to me to think that some sort of miracle might be possible, that God might not only exist but might show up in my life, or in the lives of the people whose humanity and value I was trying to acknowledge here on Skid Row?

I really didn't know. I felt like a liar. I had nothing to say for myself.

Given that this was a college spring break trip, and I have always been a good student, I had brought along a backpack full of homework. Perhaps the greatest miracle of the trip was that Kierkegaard was in that bag.

Reading Kierkegaard for the first time was like someone, somehow, had lifted a huge weight off my shoulders I barely knew I was carrying. It was the weight of logic, of certainty, of proof. Kierkegaard reframed my understanding of doubt, and showed me that not only is it possible to doubt yet remain a Christian, but that in fact it may be the only way one can become one. Perhaps his most well-known and oft referenced idea is that, in fact, without doubt there is no faith. A bit of an outsider himself, Kierkegaard seemed like a kindred spirit to a young, alienated, budding philosopher like myself. I felt that I was standing in a field alone, confronting a choice about how I would align my life. Would I give up on the church, on the God I only partially believed in, or would I press on? "Infinite resignation," Kierkegaard writes under the pseudonym Johannes de Silentio in *Fear and Trembling*, "is the last stage before faith, so that anyone who has not made this movement does not have faith, for only in infinite resignation do I become conscious of my eternal validity."[4] I was searching for this kind of resignation, and I was unsure whether or not I had it, but at least, here, was someone who understood the need for it.

4. Kierkegaard, *Fear And Trembling*, 46.

> . . . he can be saved only by the absurd, and this he grasps by faith. Consequently, he acknowledges the impossibility, and in the very same moment he believes the absurd, for if he wants to imagine that he has faith without passionately acknowledging the impossibility with his whole heart and soul, he is deceiving himself and his testimony is neither here nor there, since he has not even obtained infinite resignation.[5]

The absurd! There was the concept I had been wrestling with, the absurdity of what I believed, alongside the strange realization that I did *believe* it. Though I would later realize that Kierkegaard's treatment of faith is far from a glorification of doubt in and of itself, and not merely about the individual, that in fact the reader herself is not the "knight of faith" in Kierkegaard's thought, nor should she aspire to be, for the time being this affirmation of my reality was exactly where I needed to begin again, approaching my faith anew. "Philosophy is perfectly right in saying that life must be understood backwards," read my assigned reading that week from Kierkegaard's journals and papers. "But then one forgets the other clause—that it must be lived forwards."[6] These popular excerpts were my gateway drug, giving me the language I needed for the absurdity I felt.

On our last day in LA we rested. I sat with my friend Katherine on the beach, toes in the sand, staring out at the ocean. We were silent. Neither of us understood why we had decided to come here, yet perhaps as we let the silence hold us a little bit of spirit crept in. Instead of resignation, I felt release. We cried, without knowing exactly why.

I returned to school, burnt out on churchy things, consumed by existential angst and my pursuit of Kierkegaardian "resignation." As the semester wore on, I became enthralled by this Dane, even as I became obsessive about philosophy more generally. The devotion to Christianity that I was struggling to maintain shifted to

---

5. Ibid, 47.
6. Kierkegaard, *Journals and Papers*, V.1, A-E, 451.

my intellectual pursuits. They became a way I could wonder and wander and think about God without needing to find the right answers. I was as devoted as ever, in some respects, but I was searching for different answers. Lubbers Hall, which housed the departments of Religion, Philosophy, History, English, and Political Science, became my church—a cathedral of learning in which I could confess my doubts, and be absolved.

In those days, I still snuck into the Sunday night services in Hope College's Dimnent Chapel. I showed up about fifteen minutes late, ensuring I had missed the happy-clappy contemporary praise songs, sung with eyes closed and hands lifted to the skies. These songs irked me, not so much because I didn't believe the people around me were experiencing something in singing them, but because I wasn't experiencing whatever or whoever it was.

My school had just hired a new chaplain, Trygve, and he was a smart man—someone who would later become a friend and mentor to me, though I didn't know him personally then. "O Chaplain, my Chaplain," he once told us to call him, earning my respect with a dual reference to Whitman and *Dead Poets Society* (he would go on to form a Dead Preachers Society for those of us on campus considering going on to divinity school). Trygve seemed comfortable with my questions. So every week I would climb the stairs to the balcony as the last song played, slip into a pew, shrink down to remain as invisible as possible, and I would listen. Somehow, in all of his words, I think this thing Christians call the Word got through to me. Somehow, I heard the good news that I was lovable, worthwhile, that who I was was not dependent upon my performance—news that was as much about my ability to perform a perceived right way of being Christian as it was about basing my self-worth on my grades and other successes. There was some freedom in what he said. It was much like the freedom I felt when Jim said, in philosophy class, that it was okay to change our minds, and that our work and words mattered more than grades.

After the sermon ended, people would bow their heads to pray, and I would sneak out before communion. The total opposite of most chapel goers, I came only for the sermon—the part most students wished was shorter, the part most people struggle not to simply tune out. Once in a while I bowed my head too, though. I shifted uncomfortably in my seat, listened to the words, whispered "amen." I received the invitation to the communion table, to eat, and drink, many grains gathered into one loaf—me and my doubts alongside my charismatic classmates, my roommates, my professors. I would approach the communion servers, often with my head hanging low, overwhelmed by feelings of inadequacy, trying to grasp the love I was offered, and sometimes the server would be a friend or favorite teacher. BP—as students fondly nicknamed Professor Bouma-Prediger—always chose the words, "The body of Christ, strength for the journey" when he served, breaking off a piece of bread and pressing it into my hand, holding eye contact as long as I would allow. Whatever else those words meant, I knew that something greater than myself would sustain me, and somehow that was enough to keep going, to church as well as to philosophy class.

The following summer I started reading Kierkegaard's *Fear and Trembling* in its entirety. The book is a retelling of the story of Abraham and Isaac, in which God commands Abraham to sacrifice his only son despite the fact that God has also promised that he will make Abraham the father of a great nation. Tough to do without an heir, right? Abraham trusts God, follows the absurd command up to the last moment when God stops his hand from stabbing Isaac, who lays bound upon the alter. This passage has puzzled scholars and religious leaders for ages.

It was not great beach reading.

What is this strange faith Abraham had? Who is this God, who commands such things? Those questions would occupy me for a long time, and provoke many rereadings of the text. I packed *Fear and Trembling* in my suitcase when I left for a semester in London that fall, and continued to ponder these questions, abstractly and in my own life. I also took another philosophy class while I was overseas. My new professor, an intimidating Italian man, was no Jim Allis. I hated the class. Yet I still found the material engrossing. I studied harder in that class, an introduction to ethics, than any other that semester, discussing the material with my roommate over pints of ale at The Trafalgar, a pub down the street from our dorm in Chelsea, and when it came time to register for spring courses back at home, I made a decision: I emailed Jim and asked him what courses I should take next, and I called my parents to tell them I was changing my major. To philosophy.

This is what all blue-collar parents want to hear their first-generation college student daughter say when she is an ocean away, right? I delivered my carefully prepared speech about how philosophy prepares people for a variety of pursuits, and teaches you to think, and made sure I saved my best line for last. "It's great for people who are thinking about law school, Mom," I mentioned. I had no desire to go to law school, but I knew my mother harbored a not-so-secret belief that I would make a fine lawyer. What was the harm in soothing her nerves a little?

My parents sufficiently comforted for the time being, I enjoyed the rest of my time abroad and returned to Michigan ready to delve into my studies in earnest. That was a course load I have no trouble remembering: Existentialism, Philosophical Theology, Intro to World Religions, Informal Logic.

Soon I was barely sleeping. These lines from Kierkegaard's *Works of Love*, which I had yet to read, aptly describe my state at the time: "Which deception is the more dangerous? Whose recovery is more doubtful, that of the one who does not see, or that of the person who sees and yet does not see? What is more difficult—to awaken someone who is sleeping or to awaken someone who, awake, is dreaming that he is awake?"[7] I was searching for answers, and the search was one of both literal and figurative waking.

I shot up in the wee hours one night that I had actually managed to fall asleep at a decent hour, and lay in bed unable to return to sleep, pondering the problem of evil—that is, how can a good God allow bad things to happen? We were in the midst of a five-week study on theodicy, which is the term for attempts to answer to this question about evil, in my Philosophical Theology class,

7. Kierkegaard, *Works of Love*, 5.

and thinker after thinker came up short for me. My grandfather died while I was in the middle of reading Nietzsche for my Existentialism course at the same time, and between the idea of the *übermensch*, his theory of eternal recurrence, and the oft-quoted pronouncement that "God is dead," existential despair took on flesh and blood for me. It wasn't until week five of Philosophical Theology that I found a way to make any sort of sense out of the loss of my grandfather within months of the birth of his first great grandchild, my cousin Matthias.

Professor BP assigned *Lament for a Son* by Nicholas Wolterstorff last, and finally the whole grueling five weeks of insufficient arguments came together. Wolterstorff's book was written after the death of his son in a mountain climbing accident at the age of twenty-five. I was submerged in its honest, open grief, the raw pain Wolterstorff bled onto the page. "Grief is existential testimony to the worth of the one loved," he writes in the preface to the 2001 edition, twelve years after his son's death.[8] *Lament for a Son* is an act of grieving, and its theodicy was *lament*. That was the only theodicy I could abide.

At twenty-one, I had always prided myself on my unwillingness to allow others to see me cry. After I received the news that my grandfather was in hospice, with only a short time to live, for maybe the first time I let myself hurt in front of others. I left a message for my best friend Laura, who showed up with a plate of food from a party some classmate was having down the street, and two arms whose embrace let me dissolve into a flood of tears I would usually have held back until I was alone. Tally and Lisa came by later, ready to drive me to Kalamazoo, an hour and a half away, to be with my family immediately, even though it was getting late and we were in the middle of a cold Michigan winter. I refused, afraid of missing class the next day, not anticipating that my professors, like my friends, would be kind and supportive as I stumbled into this new grief. I let Tally and Lisa take me out for ice cream instead, went to class the next day, and then waited for my dad to pick me up so that I could go home and wait for my grandfather to die.

8. Wolterstorff, *Lament for a Son*, 5.

"You are not a thing," Jim had said the first day of Existentialism, by way of definition of our subject matter. And I wasn't. I had to start setting boundaries for my obsessions. On top of the grief of losing a family member, I also had to cope with my unrealistic expectation that in the midst of funeral preparations at home I would continue to keep up with all of my schoolwork. In Kierkegaardian fashion, philosophy was personal for me, and as another existentialist thinker, Simone de Beauvoir, put it, "In truth there is no divorce between philosophy and life." In my grief I dove in further, yet I knew I couldn't live like this forever.

Returning to school after we buried my grandfather, I was physically and emotionally spent. I needed to compartmentalize, or at the very least spend a bit more time at the local watering hole relaxing with friends. As I struggled through midterms and made plans to work at the summer camp where I had worked every summer since finishing high school, my mother finally became the voice of reason.

She asked me if I'd ever thought about taking a break.

I had not. I took her advice and turned down the camp job—notorious for seventy-hour work weeks and low pay—in favor of a gig as a summer Resident Advisor that included free rent in the small lake town where I went to school. I started to look forward to afternoons lying on the beach, and then, because summer has always meant reading for me, I set about planning a book club. A favorite history professor would later say to me that anyone who organizes a summer book club on the scale that I did was basically "doomed" to go to graduate school. Having warmed to the idea since my advisor first suggested that graduate education might be in my future, I took that as a compliment.

Together with a couple of equally bookish friends, I emailed favorite professors and asked what books each of them would suggest to students as "must reads" before graduating. We wanted to know their "best ever" book recommendations. And so the Best Ever Book Club was born.

We chose one book from each professor, created a syllabus (yes, a syllabus), and then invited the professors to join us the week that we discussed their books. We read *Madame Bovary*, *The Brothers Karamazov*, selections from Wendell Berry, and Thomas Merton's *New Seeds of Contemplation*, among other things. The Merton text was suggested by my Logic professor, Jack. He had also suggested Kierkegaard's *Works of Love*, but I had been unable to convince my friends to include it on the syllabus. They were wise to talk me down off that ledge—it is nearly 400 pages long, for one thing—but they could not hold me back permanently. The book lodged itself in my mind, a "must-read" before our graduation the following May.

Jack invited us over to his home to discuss Merton, and I met his wife Melissa for the first time. As we sat around sipping coffee she started talking about *Works of Love*, and the Kierkegaard Library at St. Olaf College. When Jack was in graduate school they spent a summer there while he did research for his dissertation, and she participated in a *Works of Love* reading group with him. She echoed my friends' sense that it would have been a bit much to include it on our summer reading list, but I was too distracted by her mention of this Kierkegaard Library to hear much else. I laughed as she told stories about being one of the only women in residence that summer, philosophy still being a male-dominated field, and how she would hang a warning sign on the door of the shared bathroom whenever she took a shower, just to be on the safe side. I tried to imagine spending a summer in a place where everyone around me shared my slowly growing love of Kierkegaard.

As summer wore on I began to think that my history professor was right—perhaps I was doomed to go to graduate school. And perhaps I would study Kierkegaard. My understanding of what that meant was still limited, however, and first I had another year of school, not to mention applications to fill out, rejection letters to cope with, and finally an acceptance to rejoice over.

Most importantly, first I had to actually read this book, *Works of Love*. Fall semester of my senior year flew by with required courses for my major and drama with my roommates, and I took a full load in my final semester so that I could complete a second major in religion. Weekends, as always, were spent doing school work at my favorite coffee shop, JP's. Best of all, I convinced both department heads that a directed study on *Works of Love* should count for both of my majors. And so my Friday afternoons with Jack began.

Jack is a tall, thoughtful, blond man, awkward in that endearing way that philosophy professors inevitably are. Born and raised in the Dutch Reformed tradition (the same one my parents had raised me in), he converted to Catholicism in college. He was the only person I knew who liked Kierkegaard more than I did. *Way* more. His office was lined with books I had never read but hoped I would, eventually—beautiful Princeton editions of Kierkegaard's works, translated by Howard and Edna Hong, secondary scholarship on Kierkegaard's works, other non-Kierkegaardian books about religion and philosophy. There was also a collection of philosopher finger puppets Melissa bought for him. On the fourth floor of Lubbers Hall, home of all my favorite professors, Jack's office window overlooked 10th Street, and in the spring, beautiful flowering trees and rocking chairs on the front porch of the campus ministries house across the street.

It was a picture of a future I was I afraid to hope for, a future as a scholar and a professor. I was twenty-two, and I finally knew at least one thing that I wanted for myself. I still wasn't sure how to get there, though. I was looking for someone to show me the way; I didn't yet know that I'd have to make it up on my own.

It had taken all my nerve to ask Jack to supervise this directed study, shy as I was, though I figured all along that he would be happy to help a student read a text he told me was one of his favorites. When the semester began, I read about fifty pages a week, because Jack thought it best to read slowly and carefully, instead of at the usual breakneck pace of many of my courses, which resulted in students remembering nothing they read—or giving up on trying to read at all. Jack knew college students well, perhaps because he was young enough to remember being one himself in the not-so-distant past. He told me that if I got stuck, I should read aloud, and so I closed my bedroom door and paced around, delving deeper into the text, getting lost, and finding my way out again. From time to time Jack would also have me read articles by contemporary Kierkegaard scholars, and each week I wrote an informal one- or two-page paper to get our discussion going.

Those discussions were the highlight of my week. Yet I also dreaded them, at times. I was still learning to articulate my ideas, and the text was dense. Besides that, I hated the thought of appearing stupid in front of a professor I respected. Those old perfectionist habits died hard. Most of the time I simply did not know what I thought yet, and compared to my normal classes, now the discussion was all on me. There was no lecture component here. It was Jack, me, and our Danish friend Søren.

There were a lot of long pauses during those discussions. Often I began by reading my short paper aloud, grateful to at least have some ideas to start things off, always more confident with my pen than with my voice. At other times I stared out the window at those rocking chairs across the street, and past them to the dorm I lived in my first year of college. "Well . . ." I said, and paused again. "I guess . . . maybe . . . it seems like . . ." and perhaps then the words started to trickle out. I started to say what I really thought, which was that Kierkegaard was right about all of this Christian love stuff. But that I worried he was also wrong, sometimes.

Kierkegaard's understanding of love begins with a central assumption taken from Matthew 22:39: "You shall love your neighbor as yourself." He goes so far as to assert that if loving one's neighbor is not a duty (e.g. you *shall* love, whether you like it or not), the concept of neighbor does not exist. He writes in his journals, "And it is this Christian love that finds out and knows that the neighbor exists and, what amounts to the same, that everyone is that, because if it were not a duty to love, then the concept of 'neighbor' would not exist either."[9] In other words, what besides duty could make sense of a person's efforts to love that neighbor whom she has no particular preference for, not to mention loving the neighbor who she flat out doesn't like? And, on top of that, without duty, loving one's enemy (a central aspect of Jesus' teaching) would be impossible; the Christian, Kierkegaard emphasizes,

9. Kierkegaard, *Works of Love*, 430.

is called to love not only the people she naturally *likes*, but even those she is tempted to hate.

These are hard words, words that I knew in theory having grown up in the church, but words that I now wrestled with philosophically and personally as I tried to make sense of duty as a concept, and the strange idea of loving someone you don't like at all. I was struggling just to love my roommates, who I genuinely liked, but who also genuinely got on my nerves a lot of the time. And while Kierkegaard's understanding of the love of neighbor assumed and rested on the necessity of self-love, so few pages of *Works of Love* were devoted to the self that it diminished in comparison to love of others.

I was only just coming to realize that I was not very good at the whole "self-love" thing, so this was more than a bit disconcerting.

Sometimes my conversations with Jack would shift away from Kierkegaard, and I would say, too, that I wanted to go to graduate school more than anything, but was afraid I wouldn't get in, afraid I wasn't smart enough. I wanted to know as much as Jack knew, though I never told him that part, or at least never in those words. Mostly I plodded through the text slowly, my teacher always patient, never filling the awkward silences with his own words, letting me think, letting me struggle to find my own opinions. When it was apparent that I disliked a certain idea we were discussing, Jack reassured me that even he was not Kierkegaardian on *all* issues.

One week I came in, completely exasperated by the excessive self-giving nature of love as Kierkegaard articulates it, and read to Jack from the paper titled, "Does loving make me a doormat?" which was my attempt at making sense of the need for self-care in my life as an RA who spent a lot of time looking after everyone else and putting other people's needs first. When I finished reading the most personal essay I had written that semester, I looked up at Jack, nervous for his response. "Meghan," he said, "not everyone can do the kind of work you're doing, and the people who can, should." I didn't know then how true that would be, nor how often I would need to return to that moment, to struggle to believe those words, a blessing spoken over my work and my goals as I left the intellectual womb of Hope College for the wider world of academia. I return to them still, and I hope they are true.

After receiving rejection letter after rejection letter, I finally got a call. I returned to my apartment on St. Patrick's Day 2007 to a message on the shared answering machine from the admissions director at Duke Divinity School, congratulating me on my acceptance to the Master of Theological Studies program. I jumped up and down on the couch in the empty apartment, squealing with glee, before calling my friends to come over and celebrate with me. That night we watched *Waking Ned Divine* and ate sticky toffee pudding, and the following morning we left for spring break. Our final semester was nearing its end, and my relationship with Kierkegaard was moving to the next level.

In August I moved to Durham, North Carolina—a state I had never set foot in before—and prepared to make my dreams a reality, bursting with optimism and ambition, plus a bucket of nerves. During MTS orientation, a one-day affair before the twenty of us joined the rest of Duke Divinity for school-wide orientation alongside 150 or so Master of Divinity students, it became immediately apparent that I had entered an alternate universe. As we went around the room and stated our research interests, I became increasingly intimidated by the in-depth research descriptions my soon-to-be classmates articulated. I liked books and theology and philosophy, and I wanted to read more Kierkegaard. I felt childish, almost cliché, listening to my new colleagues' intellectual posturing. This was nothing like Hope College. I was in the academic ivory tower now, and I had a lot to learn—much of which had nothing to do with the books I would be reading.

For starters, everyone was already worried about preparing to take the GRE before applying to PhD programs, when we had yet to register for our first masters-level courses. Then there was the small matter of finding myself suddenly in the minority as a woman after spending the last four years at an institution with a

45:55 male:female ratio. Worse than the numbers was the slow revelation of ideological misogyny that would become my new normal.

First, I met with my advisor, who sat across from me with my college transcripts laid out on his desk, showing my double major in religion and philosophy, and told me, straight faced, that I could not take the course I wanted to take on Gender, Theology & Ministry with Dr. Amy Laura Hall because I "did not have the prerequisites" (when in reality, had I asked Dr. Hall, I would have found out I had a perfectly acceptable equivalency, described in those very undergraduate transcripts on my new advisor's desk). Dr. Hall was the reason I had come to Duke; I had exactly four semesters here, and this pronouncement from above devastated me. I still trusted the authority of the institution, though, so I nodded and tried my best to get over it. Later I would notice the undercurrent of professors subtly discouraging students from academic work relating to gender. I would also observe who was more likely to be allowed to test out of core courses and skip those prerequisites that were holding me back. Genitalia had something to do with it.

Then, my church history class began, and I had to listen to my professor drone on and on whilst refusing to use gender-inclusive language. I was linguistically and theologically horrified. Even if he was not a feminist (he wasn't) there was no excuse for saying "men" when he meant humanity, in my book. It was imprecise, if not flat out grammatically incorrect, and I told him as much. I loved church history, but I couldn't wait to get out of his class and into a course with a woman, any woman.

All of this is to say nothing of the student body, nor of my attempts at a social life among young men who did not know how to talk to women except if they were considering us as potential mates. In class, I fell silent again. When I dared raise questions that critiqued the dominant male narrative of theological orthodoxy and the early church, I was shut down, told my concerns were a "side issue," a "contextual question." As if orthodoxy arose from a contextual void.

My first year, I survived. My second year, I was reunited with my beloved Kierkegaard, with a new set of feminist questions and a new mentor in Dr. Hall.

Dr. Hall was the first woman Kierkegaardian I ever had the opportunity to apprentice myself to—the SK Fan Club still doesn't include many women, and encouraging though they were of my growing interest in feminism, my undergraduate mentors were nonetheless all men. And so it was that, with her, my love of Kierkegaard and my growing interest in the intersections of gender and theology crashed into one another. An ordained Methodist minister in addition to her scholarly laurels, Dr. Hall taught theology and ethics in a way that made sense to me—a way that considered actual people, instead of only muddling about with abstract ideas. A way that took bodies and all of their implications and complications seriously.

I was still a quiet student, even in her Kierkegaard seminar. There were only fourteen of us, which was less intimidating than my larger courses, and Dr. Hall did her best to draw all of us out. She had rules about academic posturing: while most professors would let my tweed-clad male classmates drone on and on in class about thinkers who barely related to the course, without explaining them to those who hadn't read this or that book, thus shutting down real conversation for anyone who hadn't read these other, tangentially related books, Dr. Hall would shut them down. If you wanted to bring up Kant in her Kierkegaard class, you needed to be able to provide your classmates with a primer on what he was about, and how he connected to the text we were reading, or else you needed to shut your trap and let everyone else talk about the work that was actually assigned. This tendency of my classmates to hijack the discussion had contributed more to my silence than anything else. I lived with an ongoing sense that I had not read enough, did not know enough, to join the conversation. But now I was in my element, with my favorite thinker, and a professor who called people on their pretensions. It got better.

However, she also turned my world—and my understanding of Kierkegaard—upside down. We began the semester reading

Fear and Trembling, a text I had a history with. In class, as we sought to discuss it, students would begin sentences, "Kierkegaard says . . ." and Dr. Hall would interject.

"De Silentio says," she corrected. We had been taught to read him the wrong way. The popular understanding of Kierkegaard— the same one I had picked up on my own, and which had been so useful to me in college—missed the mark insofar as Kierkegaard writes under a wide variety of pseudonyms, not all of which represent his own views accurately. Dr. Hall believed understanding the relationship between the pseudonyms mattered for understanding Kierkegaard's thought, and this would become important for my ability to make sense of certain ideas in his work that began to trouble me.

I loved Kierkegaard, but when we moved on from *Fear and Trembling* to *Works of Love*, I found it even more difficult to reconcile myself to the text than I had on my first reading as an undergraduate. I came to class one September morning in a tizzy. We had read and written a short paper about the sixth section in *Works of Love*, called "Love is a Matter of Conscience," in which the following passage appears:

> Christianity's divine meaning is to say in confidence to every human being, "Do not busy yourself with changing the shape of the world or your situation, as if you (to stay with the example), instead of being a poor char woman, perhaps could manage to be called 'Madame.' No, make Christianity your own, and it will show you a point outside the world, and by means of this you will move heaven and earth; yes, you will do something even more wonderful, you will move heaven and earth so quietly, so lightly, that no one notices it.[10]

The first time I read the text, I loved this passage. I wrestled with its meaning, as well, but in the end I made some peace with Kierkegaard's sense that matters of eternal worth were more important than temporary improvements to one's worldly situation. That seemed like something Jesus would have gotten behind.

10. Kierkegaard, *Works of Love*, 136.

But now I was living in a city where I was confronted with stark contrasts between wealth and poverty, and a history of racism it has yet to leave behind. The "shape of the world" looked different to me now, and as Kierkegaard went on in this section to flippantly (or so it felt to me) state that women should not concern themselves with worldly equality because they already have the equality of the eternal—that is, men and women are equal before God—well, I simply threw the book on the floor. Literally.

It was our first big fight.

I wanted to agree with him, I really did. I wanted to say that, if one gave him the benefit of a doubt, called him a "product of his time," that would solve the problems in the text. But I wasn't quite sure that was true, not yet. This question of equality, and the tension between equality and *love*, became the driving force behind my master's thesis. Kierkegaard is adamant that before God all are equal—rich, poor, male, female, etc.—yet I couldn't understand how an inward change with no outward, visible fruits could really be the infinite change he calls for. He is equally adamant that love is recognized by its fruits, and I wanted him to tell me that meant social activism and radical feminism. Affect change! That was not his style.

That spring, as I struggled to write my master's thesis, I read and reread Theodor Adorno's Marxist critique of *Works of Love*, a long-standing argument that any scholar worth her salt has to take on if she is going to make a case that Kierkegaard's love ethic is compatible with justice and equality. I felt, yet again, like an intellectual peon. What could I say to Adorno that hadn't already been said by people much smarter than me? As I read critique after critique, I found myself sympathizing with Adorno. Maybe I was more Marxist than Kierkegaardian after all.

At the same time I was wading through another of Kierkegaard's texts for the first time. *Stages on Life's Way* is another pseudonymous work, in which Kierkegaard creates a whole cast of different characters who, I would come to argue, represent various failed ways of loving their neighbors. As I reacted emotionally to each fictional representation of love, I became convinced that

Kierkegaard's understanding of love—as articulated under his own name, in *Works of Love*—was right, despite my reservations. The pseudonyms in *Stages on Life's Way* sent me back into *Works of Love* with renewed fervor. What was I missing?

It was right in front of my face: Adorno was talking about justice, and Kierkegaard was talking about love. *They are not the same thing.* Every argument I read attempted to respond to Adorno on his own terms—but what if his terms were wrong? I cared about justice, but Kierkegaard simply wasn't writing about that. Had he written about it I would no doubt have disagreed with whatever he had to say, yet the point stood: love is different from justice, and one's ability to *love* is not dependent upon her economic situation. In this, at least, there is equality.

For my part, I was ready to fight for the other kind of equality too, but this moment of revelation was freeing: often I felt helpless in the face of poverty and inequality, much as I had in LA as a college student. I was confronted with problems I simply could not fix. While I still felt compelled to try, there was something useful in the admonition to *love*, because in that at least I was without excuse. Kierkegaard dwells on the idea of love as duty, but more specifically "our duty to love the people we see," that is, rather than searching for someone lovable, we ought to concern ourselves with being a person who loves. He writes, "We human beings speak about finding the perfect person in order to love him, whereas Christianity speaks about being the perfect person who boundlessly loves the person he sees."[11] In the end, this was the harder idea to practice, and one I would continue to struggle with long after Dr. Hall signed the cover page of my thesis, allowing me to graduate and move on to other things.

I was burnt out. On school, on Kierkegaard, on everything. I took a job as a restaurant hostess for a few months, then a position in retail, before finally settling on a job as a nanny. I wavered on my plans for a PhD. I wrote during the baby's nap times, I read fiction

11. Kierkegaard, *Works of Love*, 173–74.

and poetry and once in a while some theology—but not Kierkeg-aard. I didn't read any Kierkegaard for nearly a year.

I couldn't quit him, though. Two years after finishing my MTS, though I had no plans to pursue a PhD, I applied for a summer fellowship at the Kierkegaard Library at St. Olaf College. My mind was restless, I was tired of changing diapers, and I was trying to figure out whether or not I was ever going to follow through on my doctoral goals. Was I on hiatus, or had I quit? A month at the library seemed like it might be a good test run for future studies, not to mention the simple fact that I never let go of that initial fascination sparked by Melissa's stories. More than one night I had sat at my computer reading the Kierkegaard Library's website, wondering if or when I would be able to go. It was a career goal, sure, but mostly it sounded like *fun*. When I applied, I wasn't sure if they even accepted people without an academic affiliation, so I was honestly shocked when I was offered a spot. Someone was giving me a fellowship to study Kierkegaard over the summer? Only in my wildest dreams. I packed my bags, took a month off work, and headed to Minnesota.

There is a sign along the highway that leads to Northfield, MN, that reads, "Cows, Colleges, Contentment." Northfield is the home of Carleton College, St. Olaf College, a few cows, more than a few contented Midwesterners, and one of three Malt-O-Meal manu-facturing plants. It is also home of the Howard V. and Edna H. Hong Kierkegaard Library.

On any given day of the week, the air is sweet with the smell of Coco Roos, Berry Colossal Crunch, or perhaps Honey and Oat Blenders. Other days you get whiffs of what one can assume are the more healthy Malt-O-Meal brands. Puffed Wheat, perhaps, or Crispy Rice. When I first arrived in Northfield in June, I found the cereal-scented air charming, a little quirk of this tiny town. Alas, the novelty wears off all too quickly, and I didn't eat any cereal the first summer I spent in Minnesota.

Of course, I didn't go to Northfield for the cereal. I went because by this point I had been carrying on an academic love affair with Søren Kierkegaard since 2005. Since I first learned about the library from Melissa and Jack, I had longed to embark on a pilgrimage to St. Olaf. Outside of Kierkegaard's hometown of Copenhagen, this is the center of Kierkegaardian scholarship. I was going to be a visiting scholar as St. Olaf, yes, but really I was going to Kierkegaard Camp, as the curator, Gordon, likes to call it. In stark contrast to ideas of Kierkegaardian despair, I was the happiest young woman in the world.

It's an odd thing, spending a month in a tiny town in the Midwest, in a library devoted to a single Danish philosopher. Sure, he is known as the "father of existentialism." But perhaps for that very reason most people have never heard of him, much less read any of his extensive authorship. There are, however, those who journey from all over the world to Northfield simply because tucked in the basement of the main library there you will find the Hong's legacy of Kierkegaardian scholarship—the most extensive collection in the world, including many works Howard and Edna translated into English themselves. So much of the growth of Kierkegaard studies in the United States was made possible due to their dedicated work, and their generosity to St. Olaf.

Though the Hongs have passed away, leaving their collection to the school, the library provides a gathering place for scholars every summer. My roommates were from Russia, Norway, and South Africa. Other scholars came from Brazil, Mexico, and even Denmark. There were US scholars, too, from New York, California, Kentucky, Minnesota, Georgia, and elsewhere.

If you're thinking this is the nerdiest way possible to spend a summer, well, you are absolutely right.

My journey to Northfield began on a train in Kalamazoo, Michigan, where I'd spent a week for my sister's wedding. After days filled with nonacademic conversation, fancy dresses, and flowers, it was a relief when my mother—who made it about two pages into my master's thesis before falling asleep—took me to the train station, after a stop at my favorite local donut shop to acquire some snacks for the journey. As we said goodbye, her face lit up and she said something cheesy and motherly and lovely all at the same time, like "You get to fulfill your lifelong dream!" At any other time those words would have felt far too dramatic. On that day tears began to roll down my cheeks. I smiled, heaved my suitcase up the steps to the train, waved goodbye, and settled in to enjoy a Reese's donut and a cup of coffee on the short train trip to Chicago.

After a layover just long enough to grab lunch, I hurried back to the train station for the longest part of my trip, a eight hour train to Minneapolis. I was seated next to a high school boy on his way to a more traditional summer camp. He read comic books, and shared his candy with me, and we got on swimmingly (though I had a hunch that he thought I was closer in age to him than I am). I didn't arrive in the Twin Cities until well after midnight, and crashed at the nearest hotel. After a few precious hours of sleep, I made my way to the bus stop for the final leg of my trip. As the bus meandered around Minneapolis and St. Paul, my excitement turned to nerves. The reality of spending a month with other scholars was both exhilarating and intimidating, and these feelings were heightened by the slow, multi-step journey to Northfield. Plenty of time to worry about things. I was spending the summer with the top people in my field, discussing our research, and this made me keenly aware of my lack of a PhD. Was I ready for this?

As the city faded away, rolling green hills greeted me, lush fields, the occasional cow. I tried to quell my fit of nerves, sitting on the edge of my seat, scanning the roadside for the first signs of St. Olaf and my Kierkegaardian mecca.

And there it was. Small, unimpressive yet smart, and to me, beautiful. Sitting on a hillside overlooking the town, its old stonework gives the place a feel I can only describe as studious. It looked like home to me.

I was greeted at the bus stop by an "Ole" undergrad named Devon, who drove me and my suitcase to Finholt House, where I would be living. I paused outside the door, grinning like an idiot at the sign beside it which read, "Kierkegaard Scholars Residence." That was *me*.

Devon didn't notice—or ignored—my delight, and proceeded to give me a tour of the house, and leave me to my own devices. After a short nap, and shoving my belongings into the closet, I began the trek up the hill to campus. The unseasonable day had me sweating through my clothing long before I reached the top, and when I got there I realized I had no idea where I was going. Not one to let that stop me, I continued to wander in and out of buildings, finding the gym, and chapel, and eventually winding my way back around to the student union, where I had begun my exploration. It was then that I realized the library was right next door. Shaking my head at this exhibition of my absent-minded professor tendencies, I opened the door and stepped into the air conditioned building. I breathed deeply, and paused next to the stairway, by a sign that read "Kierkegaard Library." There was an arrow pointing downstairs. As I walked lightly down the steps, I almost expected bells and whistles—or at least a sign with some bling to let me know I was in the right place. It wasn't until I wandered down a hallway, past some offices, through a lounge where fresh coffee was brewing, and under a small stone archway that I saw the tiny bronze sign, "Howard V. and Edna H. Hong Kierkegaard Library." This was it. The library. A library I had dreamed of for years.

It was surprisingly unimpressive. Small. Somehow, though it didn't meet my expectations, my excitement level stayed high, and my nerves higher. I opened the door, avoided eye contact with the other scholars hard at work, and knocked on Gordon's assistant Cynthia's door. She greeted me warmly, and gave me a tour of the library's two main rooms. It took all of five minutes, but I had no complaints. The sight of first editions in Danish, of every dissertation ever written on Kierkegaard, of more books on his works than I knew existed was more than enough for me. There was Amy Laura Hall's book, *Kierkegaard and the Treachery of Love*. And over in another corner, multiple sets of the Hong translations of Kierkegaard's complete works, on a shelf accompanied by a Danish flag. One row was made up entirely of books that Kierkegaard would likely have had on his own shelves—a sort of replica of his own library. The next row contained the dissertations: plain blue covers with gold writing, such that you had to read them closely to see which were which.

I scanned the row casually, and there was one I knew: *Mystical And Buddhist Elements in Kierkegaard's Religious Thought*, by Jack Mulder.

Who knew where all of this would lead? But right now, my teachers were with me, telling me yet again that I was where I ought to be.

Though it felt like a sign of some sort, seeing my teachers' books on those shelves, they couldn't show me the way, not really. No matter how much wisdom they offered, their paths were their own, and mine was always going to be something else, whether I got that PhD or not. My story is my own; the truth that is true for me, the idea for which I can live and die, as Kierkegaard says—no one else can live it for me.

I never did get a PhD, though sometimes I think about it still. But I come back to the library. I study, I write, I talk about Kierkegaard with fellow weirdos gathered from everywhere you can think of and places you would never have guessed. After applying to PhD programs once, and being rejected—as is so often the case on that increasingly competitive trajectory—I knew immediately I didn't want to try again. I watched friends repeat the application process over and over, with success, and go on to live the dreams I thought were my own. But I stopped myself. I had other dreams, too.

What I didn't realize when I sat in Jack's office all those years before, looking across the street at the campus ministries house, at those rocking chairs where after our meetings I might sit in the fading afternoon light, reading a novel, welcoming a slower, quieter weekend, calming my hectic philosophical mind, was that one thing no one could teach me was how to become a person. They could nudge me along the way, put books in my hand, tell their stories, listen to me. But in the end it would be me who left Lubbers Hall and found a way to live the ideas that had brought me to life. The ideas that called me back from that precipice of doubt—doubt of the faith of my childhood, yes, but also the crippling self-doubt that so often threatened my ability to live my own life.

I don't have the job I imagined as I sat in Jack's office a decade ago, but the life I wished for was, and is, the truest story I know.

What About *Breakfast at Tiffany's*?

I grew up sandwiched between two beautiful, talented sisters, Heidi and Holly. I am the proverbial middle child, my younger sister being the baby of the family in practice if not in age, since we also have a younger brother. When you have three older sisters, the last thing you want is to be babied, so Andrew was happy to let Holly take on that role. I am close to all of my siblings, but Holly and I have always shared a kind of openness that I sometimes lack with others in my family, though we have always had our differences, as well. When Heidi got married, instead of choosing a maid of honor, she let Holly and I split the job. Holly took on the bridal shower and details of the wedding, such as helping with color choices, ordering dresses, and other things about which I am clueless. I assembled wedding favors, signed the marriage license on the big day, pinned boutonnieres, and gave a toast that struck the perfect balance between laughter and tears. We make a good team.

Our differences extend into our various hobbies, too. Holly is an amateur film buff, fascinated with the past. Her shelves are lined with classic films, many of them romances, and she prefers anything starring Cary Grant or Audrey Hepburn to most contemporary movies. Perhaps more than any other film, she loves *Breakfast at Tiffany's*. She has been known to quote Audrey Hepburn's character, Holly Golightly, and she has a poster bearing her well-known image on her bedroom wall—that perfectly coiffed updo, sparkling tiara, long cigarette holder, endearing smile.

Though I do enjoy Audrey Hepburn films from time to time, I can't say that I've ever shared my sister's fixation. Maybe it's that I am not so tall and thin, making it impossible to mimic her style, or maybe it's that I'm just too cynical about the romanticism of both old *and* new films. In any case, the first time I saw *Breakfast at Tiffany's*, when I was in college, I simply wanted to understand what all the fuss was about. I thought it might be a window into my sister's inner psyche, into the ways the two of us seemed to become increasingly different as we grew older—me reading feminist theory, attending protests on campus, cutting my hair short and spiky, Holly auditioning for the opera, perfecting her make-up techniques, and enjoying an ever-present fan club of underclass male students ready to do her bidding. I understand the Audrey Hepburn fascination on some level. I can see the allure of film stars and beauty icons, but while my sister seems to genuinely enjoy such things, I can't suppress my urge to analyze them. Not to mention that Holly has always been more fashionable than I am. She can pull off the Hepburn look with more grace than I can muster. Truthfully, there was a time in college when Holly insisted that I not go shopping without her, for fear of the horrendous choices I might make in her absence. I remember standing in an Eddie Bauer fitting room a couple of days after Christmas, showing off a cozy brown professorial sweater I'd found on the clearance rack.

"Meghan. Take off the sweater" Holly said, firmly. I dutifully complied, and left the mall empty handed.

I'd prefer breakfast around a campfire to breakfast at Tiffany's. Still, I was curious what it might be about this story line that so particularly draws my sister in. Though we have *different* taste, I think she has *good* taste. She's a smart, creative young woman who majored in music and now works as an elementary school music teacher in West Michigan. And anyway, we both love a good story.

After multiple viewings of *Breakfast at Tiffany's*, I'm beginning to understand. Sort of. The way I see it, Holly Golightly, who has transformed herself—with a little outside help—from country bumpkin Lula Mae into a desirable young socialite, can't help but be appealing to young women coming of age. Though my sister's

childhood was different from Lula Mae's, like many women trying to find their way into adulthood, she has had to make a place
for herself in the world, outside of the community we grew up in.
Holly Golightly proclaims early in the film when she first meets
writer Paul Varjak that "I've been taking care of myself for a long
time."[1] She is a strong female lead, surrounded by some bumbling
male supporting actors, and her character does what she wants
to without much concern for the judgment of others. Though the
film is far from feminist, it's a delightful experience to see a leading
lady *leading*. This aspect of my sister's attraction to this film makes
sense to me. It is a nuanced love story. Holly Golightly is a woman
with some pluck, and with complicated desires.

My sister and I didn't exactly grow up stealing turkey eggs and
running barefoot through the briar patch like Lula Mae, though.
And neither of us has to rely on men our father's age to give us
change for the powder room like Holly Golightly.

In the film, Holly's new friend Paul is financially supported
by an older woman—a *benefactor*, shall we say—whom he introduces to Holly as his "decorator." That sounds better than saying
he's her "kept man." It's Holly—whose life is not so different from
Paul's at all, really—who nudges him back into his writing, perhaps inspiring a renewed belief in himself. She asks a few probing
questions about his writing life and gives him a new typewriter
ribbon, and it seems that her simple gift does what all his benefactor's money and fancy suits can't. Thus, I find it strange that Paul
later describes Holly by saying, "She's a girl who can't help anyone,
not even herself. The thing is, I can help her, and it's a nice feeling
for a change." Paul is perceptive about Holly. As the film goes on
we'll see that she *is* scared and lonely—but no more scared and
lonely than Paul himself was when he met her. While watching
Breakfast at Tiffany's, I sometimes cringe and wonder if one of the
subtle messages one could take from this film that all "girls" are
just scared and lonely, in need of a kind man who can help them.

1. *Breakfast at Tiffany's*, directed by Blake Edwards (1961; Burbank, CA:
Warner Home Video, 1999), DVD. This and all subsequent quotations are my
own transcriptions from the film.

The answer would be yes, in the context of *Breakfast at Tiffany's*, if Paul were not so in need of help himself.

Perhaps the Holly in my life connects to Holly Golightly on this level. Perhaps she is scared sometimes, perhaps she is lonely. Those are common experiences for most human beings, and life in your twenties seems particularly daunting for young woman. I am scared and lonely at times, too. Yet my sister's admiration of Hepburn's character still stumps me, because this woman whose livelihood depends on the older men she escorts about town, who give her fifty dollars every time she goes to the powder room, could not be further from my college-educated, self-supported sister and me. As for me, Julie Andrews as Maria in *The Sound of Music* is more my style when searching for a female lead with some gumption to emulate.

Still, I admit that there is something in Holly Golightly's stylish clothing, the way she carries herself, the way she receives bad news, which seduces even me. "A girl can't read that sort of thing without her lipstick," she says as she prepares to be disappointed by a note from her Brazilian lover. She will behave like a lady, no matter what the circumstances. She is poised. She is sophisticated. She is resilient. I want to be that resilient. I feel more like Amelia Bedelia, most days. And, in fact, when the door closes behind her after a night out or a party, Holly Golightly is a bit neurotic herself. Maybe we are not so different after all.

When my sister calls me to relay the drama of her latest trip home to see our parents, including the excuses she made in response to probing questions about her love life, or when she tells a funny story about running into her ex-boyfriend, I can feel the tension between awkward realities and the calm, graceful persona she wishes to portray. While I am privy to the details of her fears and mistakes, in her daily life she makes sure her lipstick is reapplied, her hair smooth and shiny, and that she can always buy a new outfit when necessary to play the part of the sophisticated but fun elementary educator. Her walk-in closet is as big as my bedroom. She works twice as hard as anyone else in her department expects her to, directing the yearly junior high musical on top of her full-time job teaching, organizing parents to help with events, going back and forth from one campus to the other in her small school district, doing her best to keep a dying arts program alive. She spends her summers directing the music program at a camp for girls in upstate New York. Her college advisor described her as "a pillar of music education."

Unlike my sister, our heroine Ms. Golightly is totally reliant upon rich men for her money. She isn't independent. She's traded her older, southern husband for rich city men who use her to build their own egos, and perhaps think that buying drinks for her is the same as buying her for themselves. She's not quite a call girl, maybe, though she is perhaps what one might now call a gold digger. Truman Capote himself is said to have described the character he created in his novel, on which the film is based, as an American geisha. However you interpret Holly Golightly's lifestyle, no one sums up the business relationships she develops better than Mr. Arbuck in the opening scene. He pounds on her door, begging to be let in: "You like me. I'm a liked guy. You like me, baby. I picked up the check for five people—your friends. When you asked for change for the powder room, I give you a fifty dollar bill. That gives me some rights."

And yet Holly says to Paul, later in the film, "I'll buy my own whiskey, and don't you forget it!" She's caught between her reliance on her benefactors, and her desire to show she can take care of herself. "She's a phony, but she's a real phony," characters repeat throughout the film. The strength and resilience of her character is true, even if the financial resources Holly Golightly draws on are not her own. They are, in many ways, the only ones offered her. Rather than arguing over whether she is a picture of liberated womanhood on one hand, or objectification on the other, it makes more sense to say that she manipulates the resources that she has as best she can. In doing so, she creates at least an illusion of freedom for herself, if not quite the real thing.

Paul, despite living his own life of illusion, wants her to see this about herself, though he may be too daft to understand how similar he is, so caught up is he with his desire to save her from herself. But perhaps it's less complicated for him, as a published author battling the inner demons of self-doubt. He has no money, but he has a vocation and an identity. Holly Golightly doesn't have those things; she doesn't really know who she is, yet. Paul's attitude is not so different from the other men in the film at times—perhaps he feels he has rights, too. He *loves* her. When she threatens to run off to Brazil in search of rich South American bachelors, his response is to say, "I'm not going to let you do this . . . Holly, I'm in love with you."

What follows is the most well-known exchange in the film, an iconic moment:

> Paul: I love you. You belong to me.
>
> Holly: No. People don't belong to people.
>
> Paul: Of course they do.
>
> Holly: Nobody's going to put me in a cage.
>
> Paul: I want to love you.
>
> Holly: It's the same thing.

For two people who in some sense have belonged to the rich men and women around them to have such an exchange is heart-wrenching. Paul is not a "rat" like the other men in the film in that he really does love her, and as sympathetic viewers most of us probably want him to "get the girl" in the end. Yet don't we also root for Holly when she says, "Nobody's going to put me in a cage"?

"That's right Holly," we might say, "you're your own woman— a wild thing—and phooey on any man who thinks he can tame you!" Young women like to quote this line, but they conveniently leaves out what Paul says a few moments later:

> You know what's wrong with you, Miss Whoever-you-are? You're chicken. You got no guts. You're afraid to say, "Okay, life's a fact." People do fall in love. People do belong to each other, because that's the only chance anybody's got for real happiness. You call yourself a free spirit, a wild thing. You're terrified somebody's going to stick you in a cage. Well, baby, you're already in that cage. You built it yourself.

Paul is right. Or perhaps he's right and wrong at the same time. He loves her and thinks they belong to each other—but he doesn't yet know if she loves him back. He's learned a lesson about both of their lives that she hasn't become aware of yet, and his accusation of cowardice says something to me about his perception of himself, too. They were both living in cages of their own making, and now he thinks they can escape. They can provide one another a way out. They can belong to each other, and no one else.

After this speech, Holly follows Paul out of the cab into the rain, crying out for the nameless cat she'd released into the downpour only moments before. They embrace in the rain with the pitiful, drenched animal between them. This scene makes me tear up every time. Like my sister, I'm a sucker for a good love story. Like my sister, I think I am a wild thing, and tell the world no one is going to put me in a cage. And so I weep when Holly Golightly goes to Paul, when she collapses into his arms with that soggy, nameless cat.

Maybe what my sister Holly loves about *Breakfast at Tiffany's* is that it captures the awkward tension between the freedom we need and the love we desire—two things that for many women have for so long felt mutually exclusive. Perhaps what simultaneously irks me about the film is the sense of unknowing as to whether Holly Golightly really gets both. That's what I want—I want to break out of my own cage, and I want the Pauls of the world to break out of theirs too. I'd like to believe we could belong to each other without hemming one another in. Perhaps that kind of belonging is the most freeing thing of all.

These days, my sister and I are both single. A few years ago Holly was close to engaged to her boyfriend of three years. He adored her. After they graduated from college, he laid out a ten-year plan for his career, graduate school, family. She was a part of it, but ultimately it was his plan, not hers. Meanwhile, I gave up pursuing an opportunity to study in Germany for a year in order to stay in the US with the man I loved. Our relationship fell apart in the end, too; I thought I was part of the plan, but I wasn't.

So now Holly and I commiserate about the sacrifices we made for guys who couldn't love us and let us be ourselves at the same time—which is the same as saying they couldn't really love us to begin with. Perhaps they only loved their own ideas of us, ideas that sometimes felt like cages, though at other times they seemed so safe and secure. And so, now, we smile politely when people inquire about our older sister Heidi's wedding and ask, "Who's next?" We go on occasional dates, but never let anyone get too close. We do our best to avoid falling in love. We've become very good at being "just friends."

As movies so often do, *Breakfast at Tiffany's* leads us up to the moment when the characters' love is professed, and then the camera pulls back, and the music carries us to the credits. In two hours of pajama-clad popcorn eating and movie watching, we can see these two characters meet and fall in love, quarrel and make up, and the implication is that now they will live happily ever after. Holly Golightly and Paul Varjak clutch each other's drenched bodies as if they'll never let go, oblivious to the rain falling around them, as the credits roll.

When I stand in the rain, I'm standing alone. When I stand in the rain, I just get wet.

What I really want to know, and perhaps what keeps me from unapologetic love of movies like this, is what happens *next*. Holly believes in happy endings, but me? I think we're still in the middle of things.

Must Love Radiohead

I am listening to Radiohead's *OK Computer* album and I wish I could tell you that this is going to be an essay about Radiohead. It would be *cool* to tell a story about Radiohead. I would tell you about driving all afternoon with my friend Bobby, with whom I was madly in love, and the third person in our "triangle of trust," Brandy, on our way to a show after my first year of graduate school. I would tell you how we bought Pabst Blue Ribbon tallboys at the gas station down the road from the amphitheater, and drank them in the car as we sat sweating in traffic waiting to get into the parking lot. I would tell you that Brandy protested both the PBR itself and the open containers in her Prius, when she wasn't preoccupied with selling the extra ticket we had to some guy by the side of the road for twenty bucks. I would tell you that this is my favorite memory of my first summer in North Carolina.

But I'm not going to tell you about all that. Instead of waxing poetic about being young and in love at a Radiohead show, I want to tell you about *not* finding love on the internet. Allow me to introduce you to OKCupid, also known as the Google of online dating.

My sister put me up to it, you know. Or so I'll continue to claim. I hadn't been on a date in two years. She said I should put myself back out there. She had a point.

It was fun for a while. All the straight men I knew were either married, or nerdy doctoral students who were as good as married to their dissertations. It was nice to realize that there are other men out there.

At first I received some nice messages, many of which were from the kind of cute, hipster guys who might even listen to Radiohead. I also got some creepy notes that can be summed up as, "U R hot. Wanna have sex?" Occasionally undergraduates without profile pictures from the university where I work would proposition me, and I'd wonder if I knew them. Maybe someone I'd helped with a paper on Descartes or Nietzsche last semester was hiding behind the screen. Best not to think about that, though. Click delete and forget it as quickly as possible. Surely the internet could serve as a screening tool to help me sift through the creeps and find the guys who, though they might not be my "soul mate," might at least be worth spending a few hours with as I tried to make my way back onto the dating scene.

Whilden, a former parole officer who had recently moved to Raleigh on a whim, was my first OKCupid date. After sending flirtatious messages back and forth for a couple of weeks, I decided I was ready to meet him in person. He seemed smart, funny, cute—the basic generic traits that come across from an online dating profile where you have to sum yourself up in tiny white text boxes—and also not like a secret serial killer. He said he'd come to Durham, since I don't drive, and because I was nervous—I hadn't been on a date in years, and never one with a total stranger—I suggested we meet for a beer on Sunday afternoon at my favorite Irish pub, Bull McCabe's. My friend Elizabeth tended bar there, so someone would be sure to notice if I went missing.

What can I say. My mother taught me to be careful.

We had a lovely time. We talked for hours. He walked me to my bicycle when we left the pub, and tentatively approached me for a hug. I consented.

I had *fun*. Strange as it may sound, this was a revelation to me. And people did this sort of thing all the time! This going on dates, meeting near strangers for drinks, deciding whether or not to let them touch you. I had been in a serious relationship with my work—not to mention that I broadcast my devotion to feminist causes loud and clear to everyone I met—for years. I just assumed I didn't know how to date. I hadn't had much practice. But so far, so good.

At Whilden's suggestion we planned to meet again. He brought his bicycle with him from Raleigh, and we rode along the Ellerbee Creek Trail together at a leisurely pace, chatting about this and that, before pedaling down to my other favorite hangout, the local brewery, Fullsteam, which I'd suggested after discovering our shared love of craft and micro brews. We sipped beers, talked for hours again, hugged, and went our separate ways once more. It was an ideal second date. The next day, he sent me a message asking me out on a third.

I wanted to say no.

Why did I want to say no? I wasn't sure. That wasn't how this was supposed to go, was it? He was nice. We had fun. Conversation was easy. We had things in common. He wasn't scared off by my feminist rants, or my interest in theology. This should have been so promising. But when he hugged me goodbye after that second date I realized I simply didn't have any desire to kiss him.

Feeling shallow, yet realistic about my desire for that thing some people call a "spark," I headed back into the jungle of online profiles. I tried to be bold and make the first move, messaging men who piqued my interest. Based on my experience with Whilden, I was hopeful.

But from there, things got much worse. After struggling to make conversation on a couple bad dates, and receiving a lot of sexist messages, I decided I needed to expand my profile to make a few things clear about myself, to weed out the misogynists, militant evangelical atheists, and run of the mill dude-bros. As I tweaked my descriptions, I also added a line to my bio, knowingly harsh, speculating that men who answer the OKCupid "match" question "How much does intelligence turn you on?" with "A lot!" might be liars. I received this gem in response: *I think intelligence is a big turn on for most people BUT ONLY if the other person is still less intelligent than yourself so I kind of agree with you and sort of not. Who likes competing in relationships?*

In a roundabout way I think he proved my point that many men I was encountering on OKCupid were not interested in a woman who they perceived as smarter than themselves. I read this, and similar messages I've received, as meaning that intelligence in a woman is a turn on, so long as "intelligence" means a willingness to listen to one's date mansplain without dissenting, contributing understanding nods of approval from time to time. Actual intellectual engagement is not required or even desirable—at least not to most of the men of OKC.

I started to wonder, too, what caused this person to jump from "intelligence" to competition? Who said anything about competing? The question was did they like smart women, not if they want someone who can dominate them in Scrabble. My dates might claim that they found intelligence a turn on, but when prompted to explain what my master's thesis was about, or even just to talk about the books I've been enjoying lately, I could see their eyes begin to wander. While I desired a conversation partner, my dates seemed less interested in talking with me than talking *at* me.

Oh, don't think I didn't try dating men who don't measure their manhood by the number of letters after their names or books on their shelves. I didn't want to judge men based on their level of education, so I considered whether the answer could be found by dating men who were less interested in intellectual pursuits, men with different interests from mine, so that we could share new things.

Sadly my experience with the lesser educated men of the internet fared no better. Usually I ended up chatting with the kind of guy who thinks he knows everything about philosophy because he read a book by Camus in high school. The rest of the time I met men who simply didn't care. Given the option, I'd choose the latter, but what did that leave for us to talk about? If they were not interested in religion or philosophy, I realized we'd eliminated most of what I find interesting before we'd even met. The intellectual guys didn't know how to talk to me, but did I know how to talk to anyone else?

Lately I find myself wondering if my degrees ruined me for dating "ordinary" men. I do have other, less intellectual interests, but a quick look at one of OKCupid's blog entries on profile trends while doing my dating research one day implies that perhaps even those non-academic interests might leave me stranded in a dating wasteland. The top words and phrases in white women's profiles (i.e. my own demographic) include the following words and phrases: mascara, Nicholas Sparks, horseback riding, I'm blond, Kenny Chesney, Diet Coke, my toes, and baking. My profile talks about Kierkegaard, feminism, literature, politics, craft beer, folk music, hiking, soccer, and bicycling. Who are these Diet Coke- and toe-loving bakers, I wonder, and have they had better luck with online dating than I have? If I just learned to care about mascara, and liked Kenny Chesney, would all of this be easier?

I sifted through the messages I received one week, in search of someone with my new basic standard of humble but interesting, and found myself spending that Saturday evening with Jason, who doesn't like any sports or outdoor activities, and also doesn't care about politics (not mention that he had never heard of Kierkegaard). We had very little to talk about. I pulled conversation topics out of thin air, trying to ask intelligent questions about computer science, his chosen field, giving thanks that he was at least well-mannered and nice to look at. After I waxed poetic about the brewery in my hometown for a few minutes upon discovering their lager on tap at the bar where we perched waiting for a table, he said, "So, you seem like a heavy drinker."

After that one I thought I should start writing a microblog called "Things You Should Never Say to a Woman on a First Date." I missed Bobby, and those backseat PBRs, more than ever.

Anyway, I knew it would never go anywhere when (after I ordered a pint of my beloved Lager of the Lakes) he told the bartender he'd have "whatever you recommend." I didn't think I could date a man with no opinions about beer, though based on that criteria I suppose Jason might have been excused for his assumption about my drinking habits.

Meanwhile, OKCupid delivered new matches to my email inbox. They informed me that it was raining in Durham, and more people sign on to OKCupid when it is raining, making this the perfect time to message that special someone. (A rainy Saturday night. The perfect time to seem alone and desperate?)

Then I received this beauty: *how are you are u get alot of rain yet?*

That is the best you can do? All I ask is a little effort. And I'm sorry no one told you that "alot" is the one spelling mistake I consider a deal-breaker in a potential date. At least spell out full words. I'd like to think I'm worth an extra minute or two of your time when composing a message, though at this point in the game it didn't take much to set me off, I admit. OKC was succeeding in one thing: teaching me to read between the lines.

It's all quite sad when you think about it. The internet allows me to reject men before I even meet them. Granted, they are probably rejecting me at a similar rate (possibly for less substantive reasons than spelling and grammar).

Which brings me to my least favorite OKCupid feature: "Quickmatch." Personally, I refuse to use quickmatch to rank people. But every once in a while I get an email like this: *Smart-Girl1234, someone chose you! He's totally into you! Go send him a message. You got this email because he rated you 4 or 5 stars.*

Quickmatch is a "game" where you rank people based on a short summary of their profiles, plus a picture. You assign a numbered rating, a score of 1–5 stars. If someone has a theory as to how this could be about anything other than surface issues such as who is the hottest (whatever the objective scale of hotness refers to), please enlighten me. Note that OKCupid never tells you whether your ranking was actually four or five.

Either way, I am not flattered. I'm offended.

It is as if I have been transported back to a high school experience I never even had, but heard about or watched in movies, where neckless football players with tree trunk legs sit on the bleachers and holler numbers at the young women who walk past. Somehow this image is imprinted in my mind, and it doesn't even matter whether it happened or not. The only difference between this adolescent movie in my head, and twenty-something reality is that now the top score is a five, instead of a ten. The anger and humiliation are the same.

It will never matter how we are ranked, because what kills us is that we *are* ranked in the first place.

For me, this raises all sorts of questions about the way men's perception of women has been so clearly warped when they rank us like show dogs, or prize-winning horses. Right now, though, I'd be happy if I could just figure out why dating is so damned confusing.

Clearly we've got issues. We live in an era characterized by renewed backlash toward feminism, even as young, diverse groups of new feminists are struggling to make themselves heard. We still have people like Phyllis Schlafly, who is quoted in an interview with Hillsdale College as saying, "Feminists are the source of most problems today." From another point on the anti-feminist spectrum, Maxim magazine recently published a spread on "How to Cure a Feminist," the contents of which I'd rather forget. If feminism at its most basic is simply the affirmation of women's humanity, and the equality and rights that go along with that, something is wrong with this picture.

All things considered, dating as a feminist was beginning to feel almost impossible. It also seemed not quite worth worrying about, what with all the other problems women encounter. Yet I couldn't help but think that if we want to reimagine gender dynamics on a large scale, dating is probably important, too. There is little precedent for straight single women in their twenties as to how to date while feminist, despite how many women have done so before us. The rules of the dating game seem largely unchanged.

As you can see, I am a curmudgeonly participant in the world of online dating, though I try to hide it in my carefully composed (and spell-checked) profile. Not infrequent generic replies about how "delightful," "smart," "amazing," and "laid back" I am seem to imply that I've succeeded. Perhaps too well. Every once in a while, a message comes along from an interesting man with a decent photograph (not, for example, a headless shot of impeccable abs, nor an endearing photo of him with his ex) and passable grammar, so I will click on over to his profile. He seems nice enough after a quick skim, so I scroll up to the "The Two of You" tab at the top.

This is an important step. Months of online dating have taught me to go here as quickly as possible, and check out his match questions. These are multiple choice questions on topics ranging from ethics to sex to lifestyle to just plain ridiculous. Based on any two people's answers, OKCupid's algorithm assigns three percentages: Match, Friend, and Enemy. What these numbers really mean and how they come up with them is something of a mystery to me. In any case, though I don't have many deal breakers, surprisingly few men pass the test.

Two common scenarios occur when I check these percentages:

First, I note that we have a low "Enemy" percentage. Say 2%, for example. Upon short-cutting directly to the tab marked "questions with unacceptable answers," however, it immediately becomes apparent that he either believes in a rigid gender hierarchy where men are the head of household (thus he won't jive with my feminist consciousness), or he hates any and all even vaguely religious people (which would include *me*, the theologian). I may match him on 98% of things, but the remaining 2% is, shall we say, *problematic.*

At other times, upon scrolling to the top of the page, I'm shocked to see that "The Two of You" has morphed into "Y'all Got Issues." This is how I learned that when you are over a certain percentage "Enemy," OKCupid informs you in this not so subtle way. I'm grateful.

I am also convinced that the person who messaged me did not actually bother to read my profile.

I confess, I am as confused as you may be as to what the point of all of this is. Dating. Online dating. Writing about dating and online dating. Feigning interest in men who clearly don't have enough interest in me to even bother reading my fairly concise online dating profile. (Omit needless words, right? I do my best.)

I think that my point is that there is no point. Online dating is supposed to make things easier, but maybe it makes things harder. I can peruse the Google of online dating, and come up with a whole lot of nothing. I can go on lots of dates, and be no happier—maybe less happy, in fact—than I was during that two-year dry spell. Quantity doesn't mean quality. Furthermore, while it's nice to know that there are actually single men out there, let's not pretend everyone on OKCupid is single. The best match I've come across lately is a twenty-eight–year-old married man. OKC has shown his profile to me umpteen times, and he keeps getting cuter, but seriously, when did things get so bad that I'd date someone else's husband?

I don't even believe in "The One" that every bright-eyed young woman in my dorm in college talked about, but if I'm going to go to the trouble—and it should be clear by now that it is a great deal of trouble—of trying to date, personally I'd really like to end up with a significant other who doesn't have significant *others*. Otherwise, I'll stick to my nights in with NPR and the cat. It's like a second job trying to find one decent date. And after you've found him, you've got to sort out whether—as a feminist—it's okay to let him pick up the tab (which, in my experience, he will likely want to do). This is, of course, only the first in a series of more serious questions that will play out if you continue down this road.

Really, all dating websites do is expedite the process. The problems remain the same. Where else can you find out, within moments, that a person both supports the death penalty *and* believes women have an obligation to shave their legs? It's brilliant. Except that it's not, because while there are some things—like the death penalty, and mandatory shaving—that are deal breakers, there are a lot of other things that, if I loved someone, I am sure I could learn to live with. People do crazy things when they're in love, and I have yet to see how OKCupid can account for that—besides existing in the first place, because of course using the internet to find dates is a rather crazy thing in and of itself.

So crazy that it actually works sometimes. I think of these as the urban legends of online dating. *Everyone* knows *someone* who met someone online and is now happily married with two kids and a dog and a lake house in Wilmington.

This is part of what drives us to online dating sites: the cult of married people. Yes, there's the hope that it might work, that maybe we're one of those crazy lucky ones. Yet aren't all "happily married" people kind of crazy lucky? Isn't meeting someone you want to share your life with, forever, kind of crazy and lucky? I've found myself wanting to show up to my married friends' parties with a date once in a while just so that people know they don't need to feel sorry for me. Look, I can get a date if I want one! But see how lame he is? That's why I choose to stay single. Celebrate my fabulous single life with me! I'm like Carrie Bradshaw, with fewer shoes and more education.

Meanwhile, my married friends are reluctant to go out on Friday nights. They'd rather stay in and play board games with their spouses, I guess, so I stay home and watch a documentary with the cat, and laugh when I receive a new message from some guy whose face is cut out of his profile picture who would like to know if I am interested in having sex—er, I mean, dinner—sometime.

Please, I implore you, tell me *why* we do this to ourselves.

I really do believe it makes dating more difficult, not less. Instead of things happening organically, we put all of this pressure on one another. We try to answer the right questions in the right way, and the question has to arise as to whether we're answering them honestly. We are trying to present the best side of ourselves, sending all our wants and needs, our strengths and weaknesses, out on the internet and hoping for a top hit on some search engine.

But when I think about that June afternoon, listening to Radiohead, stuck in traffic, sipping a twenty-four–ounce can of Pabst Blue Ribbon in the passenger seat of Brandy's car with Bobby in the back, I know that love doesn't work like that. I remember that somehow I knew Bobby and I didn't have a chance in the long run, that he saw me as a friend and always would, yet that I still thought it was worth a try. And even though I have long since fallen out of love with him, I still think that was true. I'm glad I tried. I'm glad I loved him, even though he couldn't sit still long enough to really see what a gift that love was, even though he was in so many ways like a child playing with a shiny, fragile object until it fell to pieces in his hands.

When we met, I had said I'd never date a man who smokes, yet I suddenly found myself bumming cigarettes so that I could talk with him on the balcony at a party—a party I only went to because I knew he'd be there. I said I didn't like southern accents, but there I was blushing as he said my name with a hint of a southern drawl. He loved Kurt Vonnegut, and that summer I read three of his novels, writing letters back and forth to Bobby while he was away for an internship, tucking copies of my favorite Wendell Berry essays in and signing my name with a smiley face where I wanted to put a heart. We were "just friends," after all—though *he* signed his name with a heart, sometimes. When Bobby failed Greek, he was the only person I'd tell how close I'd come to failing myself. I think I loved him because for once I'd found someone who wasn't intimidated by my intelligence, but who didn't care that I wasn't as smart as I pretended to be. I think I loved him all the more because he wasn't what I was looking for, and sometimes I think love is like that.

There's no algorithm for the way he made me feel, and I wouldn't want there to be. I am cynical—about soul mates, about marriage, about prince charming, and yes, about online dating. But I do believe in love, and a quickmatch is no substitute.

A Few More Miles

It never gets easier, you just go faster.

—GREG LEMOND

After my father's stroke, after months of rehab, after coming to terms with the fact that the blind spot on his right side—his lost peripheral vision—was the new normal, his doctor told him he could no longer ride his bicycle.

Last fall he had had aortic valve replacement surgery to fix a heart condition he was born with, the same condition that ultimately killed his own father. The surgery went according to plan. They didn't know he suffered a stroke until two days later, when he had recovered enough from the anesthesia for someone to notice that he was acting funny. In the aftermath of his surgery, and the stroke, my father says his heart is twenty years younger—but I know that twenty percent of his brain is gone forever.

He lost his ability to work his job of twenty-nine years, he lost a good bit of short-term memory, which forced him into an early retirement, and now this, his love of bicycling, this too was going to be taken away from him.

I have a picture from early September, before the surgery, of my parents at Scooter's, an ice cream shop they like to ride to together on a black Burley tandem they've had since I was a kid. They celebrated their thirty-fifth wedding anniversary with a bike ride and two giant sugar cones. My mom held hers in the air, as if giving a toast. Dad did the awkward selfie lean, trying to get them both in the picture.

And what now?

After a winter of too much TV, daily walks around the neighborhood no matter how cold it was, painstakingly typed comments on my Facebook page because of how slowly his writing skills are returning, I was afraid he would give up. My father, this man who called me on his fifty-eighty birthday and told me he'd set out to ride fifty-eight miles in honor of the occasion, but tired out and only rode fifty—this man who had ridden every single mile of two coast-to-coast bicycle trips, from California to North Carolina—this man would become a couch potato, I feared. He would sit at home and watch Fox News all day.

Greg LeMond was the first American to win the Tour de France. It was 1986. I was two years old. This was before Lance Armstrong became famous, and then infamous; before helmets were required, before all of the doping scandals. Back when hardly anyone in the United States was paying attention to the tour.

I grew up admiring LeMond, though. Every summer my dad and I would sit on the couch in our family basement and watch the tour, me cheering for whoever my dad favored that year, English journalist Phil Liggett's voice synonymous with quality sports commentary in my mind. As a child I was carted around the Midwest to road races, too, cheering for my dad from a big orange blanket along the sidelines. There were usually children's races, and when I was old enough I rode my pink tricycle down the short, straight course at one of them. I pushed those black plastic pedals as hard as I could, my chubby little legs pumping up and down. I received a bronze medal strung on red, white, and blue ribbon, and ate pink cotton candy with my family to celebrate.

When I was six, I got a pink two-wheeler for my birthday. It came with training wheels, but soon Dad was teaching me to get along without them. He'd run behind me, holding onto the seat for moral support, and then he would let go, and I would fly down the sidewalk, skidding to a stop with the coaster brakes when I reached the corner, waiting for him to help me cross the street and begin again.

The joy that pink bicycle brought to my childhood is not so different from the joy bicycling has continued to bring me throughout my life. There have been many family vacations spent camping and riding, afternoons pedaling around with friends in the neighborhood where I grew up, escapes from campus on warm afternoons in my small college town. There has always been a bicycle in my life.

When I graduated from college and moved to North Carolina, I had never owned a car, or even had a driver's license. Everyone thought now that I had a college degree in hand surely I would grow up, learn to drive, and buy a vehicle like any self-respecting adult in North America. I was about to begin graduate school in theology, though, and the idea of buying a car seemed laughable to me. I didn't want to drive, and never had, which was why I hadn't gotten a license in the first place when I turned sixteen. Instead I sought out an apartment that was within walking distance of campus, the grocery store, and a coffee shop, arguing that those were the only places I was likely to hang out for the next two years anyway. That proved mostly true.

Graduate school didn't last forever, though, and when I finished my masters degree I took several part-time jobs, and no longer had time for walking and waiting at bus stops. When my parents came down for graduation Dad spent an afternoon on the porch with the old purple commuter bike he and my mom got me when I was fourteen. He overhauled the drivetrain, trued the wheels, and added a rack on the back that I could attach panniers to for carrying my groceries. It was everything I needed in a reliable vehicle. Then he presented me with a Duke-blue tire pump with a big bow on it. My graduation present.

The transition to commuting daily was not entirely smooth; there are obstacles ranging from flat tires to fitness to inclement weather. Few things make me want to stay in bed more than waking to the sound of rain on the rooftop in February. If the temperature is below forty I may even start wishing that I had a car.

I get up anyway. I make coffee. I check Weather.com. I forgo a shower, because it never seems worthwhile when I know I will be doused with rainwater shortly. I put extra socks and shoes in my waterproof courier bag, pour what's left of my coffee in a thermos, and tuck that in the bag as well.

Donning a navy blue raincoat, black nylon pants with velcro at the ankles, and my oldest sneakers (which smell like wet dog from previous soakings), I am out the door into the rain. I swing my leg over the crossbar of my white road bike, and push off down the street. The drops fall freely, without concern for the inconvenience they've caused me, weighing down my long hair, obscuring my vision. I live near a golf course, and the long, flat stretch of road that runs alongside it presents a different view every morning. On bright, chilly winter days I watch the sky turn pink and orange through the tree line as the sun rises. On humid days my eyes pick out benches and sand traps through the dense fog. In summer, I see early risers getting in a quick game before work.

On rainy days the course is abandoned. In the early morning dampness, everything looks a brighter shade of green. The air is clean and invigorating as I start to pedal harder, moving toward my destination by the strength of my own legs. I have been dreading this since I woke up, yet it is never as bad in actuality as it seemed from the warmth of my apartment.

Bicycling is hard work, and especially in the summer that work induces sweat. In four years of bicycle commuting, despite lots of sunscreen, I've watched my face become more and more freckled. I've chosen to ignore catcalls induced by skimpy clothing, because when they heat index is over 100, who really cares what the guy I pass each day on 9th Street has to say about my legs? I haven't the energy. I'm focused on movement, labored breaths, the feel of the sun beating down on my back, and the heat radiating from the pavement when I stop at a red light.

I'm picturing Greg LeMond riding into Paris, and I am willing myself to keep going, to beat my only competitor, the voices inside my own head.

Grow up and get a driver's license.

It's unattractive for a woman to be so sweaty all the time.

We live in a car culture; get used to it.

Cycling isn't safe in cities in the United States.

Why aren't you in better shape after four years of this?

This one runs through my head every time I ride up a street with a respectable hill. It never gets easier.

Not long after LeMond's historic win in 1986, he was injured in a hunting accident on a trip with his uncle. He survived, with the addition of thirty shotgun pellets inside his body, and spent two years in recovery before his career picked up again. He went on to win the Tour de France twice more, in 1989 and 1990. LeMond was among the best in the world, yet most people in the United States didn't know who he was. Oh, sure, he was on the cover of Sports Illustrated after his come back in '89, but what about all of those years leading up to that? Years when people believed that American cyclists would never be able to compete with Europeans? His victory in '86, the first ever for an American cyclist in eighty-five years of the Tour de France, happened in relative obscurity when compared to the fame that later followed Lance Armstrong. LeMond was never a celebrity in that way.

Most of life is like that. The goals we set, the things we care about, what we hope to accomplish—very few people will see them. Training rides, weight lifting, junior races—LeMond did these things like every other racer, building his career one day at a time. Cycling, even as a commuter, is a mental game as much as any competitive sport I have ever played. When I am sticky with sweat, when my mouth is dry, and my muscles burn and I want to quit, I think about LeMond after that accident, and the pain of getting back on a bicycle after physical trauma, when people said he was finished. I think about LeMond racing and *not* winning. And then, I think about a poster on my brother's bedroom wall of LeMond sprinting for the finish line at the 1989 World Championships, two European riders on his wheel, in the rain. His muscles bulge, wet hair is plastered to his forehead, and his mouth hangs open as if releasing a battle cry. His eyes are focused straight ahead, on the finish line. He is going to get what he came for.

As I pedal up these modest hills in North Carolina's Piedmont, I have to fix my eyes on the road ahead and keep pedaling. Life is a stage race like the tour, not one all-out sprint or time trial. There are days of sun and days of rain; wins and losses; successes, failures, and recoveries.

Someday I will lose him.

That is the thought most present since the stroke. That, and he is still here. We get to keep him, for a while.

Death, mortality, finitude—these are not new concepts to me. I have pondered their meanings philosophically. I have experienced the yawning chasm of loss. My uncle, Steve, when I was in sixth grade: heroin overdose. My other uncle, Joe, when I was in eigth grade: liver failure due to alcoholism. My seventeen-year-old friend Ryan: car accident, gravel, tree, the curve of a road that led not to the endless possibilities of life beyond high school, but to one final ending for him, confusion and grief for the rest of us. But these losses never prepared me for the reality that someday I will lose my own parents.

Since the stroke my father has been more open. He cries easily now. He simply cannot hold certain emotions in any longer. Home in Kalamazoo for Thanksgiving, I sat in a chair across from him while my sister played the grand piano in the living room. A month after his surgery, the scar across his chest was still pronounced, his heart healing while the rest of his body was in limbo. Tears filled his eyes, and I watched him blink them back in what appeared to me a silent denial and quiet sorrow, and also, somehow, gratitude. He could have died. He knows this. Instead he is sitting here, listening to his daughter play piano, as he has so many times before.

"I cry more easily since the stroke," he told me on the phone last week, verbalizing what I have already seen. He says it like it's a physical side-effect, and though I don't know much about medicine I assume this is his way of explaining displays of emotion previously so out of character. Before this, there was only one time I remembered seeing my father cry, and one when I heard it in his voice over the phone and tried to ignore it.

The first time was after we packed up the Volvo to drive to North Carolina the summer I moved to Durham for graduate school. My clothes and books and a few stray boxes of kitchen stuff were packed tightly into the trunk, my cat was in her pink carrier in the back seat, drugged up for the long drive, and Dad had loaded my bike onto the roof rack. He, my mother, the cat, and I would be road-tripping down, and then they would drive off and leave me in a city and state I had never laid eyes on before, where I didn't know a single soul.

In the driveway he told me he was proud of me. I politely pretended not to see the tears in his eyes, while more welled up in my own.

And then there was the night before his surgery, when he called me.

It was only in the weeks right before the surgery that its seriousness took hold of me.

They will break his sternum, I thought. *They will cut open his heart. They will break him open, and will they be able to put him back together?*

On the phone that night before the surgery he tried to hold his voice steady, but I could hear everything he wasn't saying, everything I wasn't saying, in the tremor of his voice. A friend was picking me up as I said goodbye; she and I were going to our favorite brewery for a drink. I was in a hurry, and I felt guilty about that, but I also think now that it wasn't just about getting where I was going but about my inability to fathom my own fear that this conversation could be the last one I ever had with my father.

It wasn't. And yet, it was the last one I ever had with that version of him. They cut him open, they sewed him up, they gave him back to us—but he will never be the same.

If you spoke with him, you might not know that anything is wrong. His short-term memory was the primary loss; most of the other difficulties have been overcome, gradually, with therapy. So he pauses mid-sentence, dancing around the word he wants but cannot find, his brain trying to form new pathways where the old ones have been erased—trying and sometimes failing, though succeeding more often now than in those first few months. Still, it isn't enough. The loss of memory, and the loss of sight on his right side, lead to the loss of his job. He is only fifty-nine, and was not ready to retire.

We used to talk about how someday, when he *was* ready to retire, he would come down to North Carolina and we'd take a bike trip together. Bicycling has become the glue to our relationship, which has been difficult as I've become an adult. I don't see eye to eye with my parents on much when it comes to politics and religion, and though they are supportive of my work, my art, my impractical career choices, and graduate degrees, there is a breach between us that sometimes feels impossibly wide.

A couple summers ago I rode on the back of the tandem with him for the first time. It was a strange experience, riding a bicycle and not being the one in control of steering it. I told my mother when we got home that he was the only person I could imagine trusting enough that I would be willing to give up that control. He's been cycling for decades, and I trust his experience. Also: I am his daughter.

Riding the Blue Ridge Parkway is a dream of mine, and I thought one of these days perhaps we'd do it together. He rode sections years ago on those coast-to-coast trips—another thing I dream of doing, though I've known for a while that he probably didn't have a third one in him. But part of the parkway—that I always thought we could do together.

I guess he couldn't take it anymore.

He didn't listen to his doctor. He trusted the fact that he has ridden the same routes in Kalamazoo for decades, that his favorite route is all right turns. He chose to believe that he could learn his new limits, and that even though he'll never be able to drive again, he could learn to bicycle once more.

In April, on the first day he rode, he posted on Facebook, grammar and spelling only slightly jumbled, that it was the best day since his heart surgery six months before. The best therapy he could ask for, he said. His heart was ready for this.

But his eyes may not be. Yes, six months after surgery he rode his bike. I did not believe that would ever happen again. But even in my joy I knew that this was not a step on a brilliant recovery narrative. His eyesight is not coming back. These limitations are here to stay. And so he will adapt. He will have to limit himself. And many of our plans will not fit within those limits.

He tells me how he double and triple checks before crossing busy streets. How, because of the way his vision was affected by the stroke, cars look closer than they actually are. We take comfort in this—better that they appear closer, making him overly cautious, than the other way around.

He rides with friends, some new, some old. They look out for him. And yet, he tells me, one day a couple weeks ago he started to cross an intersection and stopped at the last minute when he realized there was a car coming he'd missed the first time he scanned. He stopped in time.

But it scared him. It scared me, too.

I would never tell him to stop riding, though. I cannot. I cannot bear the thought of losing him, but I will lose him either way—the father that I love will waste away if he cannot do this, of that I am sure. And I would rather he take this risk in order to live than that he give up and tumble into despair.

My father worked, too hard, for many years. He coached my soccer teams, went to all of my figure skating competitions, worked third shift and overtime so that my siblings and I could have the education and opportunities he did not have.

I wanted him to have the retirement he planned on, and that is gone now.

Today, he will go to occupational therapy. Today, he will check Facebook, and "like" the link to my latest blog post. Today, he will say something political that I disagree with and I will choose to ignore it because I love him too much to fight anymore. Today, I still have my father, and I don't much care about brilliant recovery narratives, climbing mountains, or triumphant entries into Paris.

I will never get on the back of that tandem with him again. I will never ride the Blue Ridge Parkway with him. But maybe, next time I am at home in Michigan, we will take a spin out to Scooter's. We will ride together a few more miles.

Life Improvement

There may come a time in an unmarried woman's life when she admits that, while her friends' kitchens sport shiny cherry red Kitchen Aid mixers (retail: $229.99), if she wants to use her own kitchen for something other than grilled cheese sandwiches and quesadillas, she's going to have to buy the accouterments herself. Some of us can make it a decade or more before we give up that trusty single frying pan and start nesting in earnest, even if the only ones settling into those nests are ourselves. Some of us remain loyal to thrift store kitchenware long term. Me, I'm one of the weak ones.

Specifically, I have a weakness for kitchen gadgets and the food they prepare.

This past summer I reached my limit. The resulting domestic blitz led me to a place I never expected I would go, a place I had mocked, in part to mask my own fear: it led me to my first IKEA experience. Note that I call it an experience, rather than a mere shopping excursion, because this how IKEA works. This is how IKEA is designed. You do not just swing by an IKEA store to pick up a few things. You do not merely go shopping at IKEA. IKEA is an event.

The Scandinavian furniture company is famous for relatively affordable assemble-it-yourself furniture. I first encountered their products when studying abroad in London, where my entire dormitory was furnished with lightweight, brightly colored IKEA couches, chairs, coffee mugs, and so forth. Emerging adults like many of my friends, not quite ready (or able) to invest in expensive solid oak bedroom sets or dining room tables, particularly given the frequency with which many of us move at this stage in life, are drawn to both the affordability and the movability of the simple pieces IKEA sells. Their furniture is not the stuff of family heirlooms, but it is a step up from the bean bag chairs and thrift store finds of college and graduate school apartments. It enables us to put certain markers of "adulthood" on our small houses and apartments, to have seating for visitors, and more than two place settings of dishes.

This much is characteristic of simple young adults shopping for furniture, homemaking for their budding adult lives. Yet IKEA gets at something deeper. From the moment you pull into the parking lot, it is as if you have entered a theme park for adults playing house. You enter the store, and have to find a map to orient yourself, not only to where things are, but where even to enter the showroom. Once you've figured that out, there is a literal path marked out, a series of rooms with different items—housewares, bedroom, living room, kitchen, linens, and so on. Taking the idea of the "floor model" to the next level, you can walk through entire IKEA kitchens, which you can buy in pieces and take home, replicating them in your own home. You thought you wanted that cute blue enameled kitchen cart, but now you see everything that goes with it, and what you want is not just a way to organize your utensils, but the ability to mimic this picture of well-organized, tastefully decorated domestic bliss. Classic advertising techniques are embodied in each carefully ordered aspect of the IKEA experience; one gets the sense that perhaps the company itself believes its own message. Even the recording playing over the speakers around the store echoes this sense that when one enters an IKEA one is doing more than just shopping. Every ten minutes or so a message about the IKEA "Life improvement project" filled my ears, a constant reminder that at IKEA, you're not just buying a futon—you're buying a life.

For my friend Kara and myself, the IKEA experience began a month in advance. Since we live two and a half hours from the nearest IKEA store we needed to find a full day that both of us had free to make the trip. We also needed to rent a truck, because I wanted to buy a futon and Kara wanted some sizable kitchen shelving. Having settled into an apartment I liked in a town I hoped to stay put in for a while, it felt like the time to pick out some new furniture that I actually *like*, instead of just repainting my thrift store kitchen table for the third time to jazz it up. While I love my eclectic collection of secondhand treasures, there were some holes in my home furnishing I wanted to fill. Aesthetically, I just wanted stuff that matched for once in my life. Thus we settled on a day, Kara made the arrangements for the truck—I don't drive, so those duties fell completely to her—and we cultivated our online shopping lists in preparation.

Kara turned forty this year; I turned twenty-nine. We both found ourselves at a crossroads in life in different ways recently— new school programs, new jobs, finally doing the things we really want to do, and settling into new homes with plans to stay put. We were nesting, though there weren't and won't be any babies on the way.

As unmarried women, even a decade or so apart in age, we had something in common: no one ever furnished our homes with the proverbial Kitchen Aid mixers, spatulas, serving dishes, and linens. Adult unmarried women—at least those in the lucrative fields of theology and creative writing, like us, who are unlikely to simply go out and fulfill our own "registries" with our own money—generally get by with family hand-me-downs combined with a few choice items purchased on sale at Target. It is difficult to make "homemaking" a priority when you're moving from one state to another for school, with a questionable timeline before the next move, especially when you can't really afford to buy furniture anyway—much less fancy kitchen gadgets—even if you were planning to stay a while.

On the edge of thirty, well out of college and used to being on my own, I've gotten tired of living this way. I am tired of this sense that I am sentenced to some sort of extended adolescence (a phrase that I have often heard thrown around in think pieces about the "Millennial" generation I am supposedly part of) because my domestic life is still so scattered. It is frustrating to be the only person in my social circle who, when inviting people over for dinner, has to borrow plates and silverware because I only own four place settings. I give thanks that at least I have those four, which my mother bestowed on me when I moved into my first apartment at the age of twenty-one, insisting that one needn't be married to start eating off glass plates instead the plastic dorm-ware I'd been using. After all, the simple fact of the matter is that the only reason my friends of my own age—and even, increasingly, those who are much younger than me—have more kitchenware than I do is that *they got married.*

As if it's not enough that they found true love, now I also have to buy them a set of mixing bowls.

In the years since I graduated, and my friends began to wed, I have dutifully attended one wedding after another, purchasing the requisite goods from each registry. There have been bridal showers, as well. And lately, baby showers. I celebrate each of these significant life transitions with my friends, whom I love, and I have never needed to fake the joy I share at these events.

But why, oh why, must each and every one be marked by another gift registry? And why must I furnish everyone else's kitchen but my own?

Especially disheartening in this context is the fact that I love to cook, and to share meals with others. Yet my lack of material goods needed for entertaining leaves me feeling like somehow my adulthood doesn't count. (I don't even have more than two matching water glasses, for goodness sake.) The table I got for fifteen dollars at Goodwill when I moved to North Carolina for graduate school six years ago, and the 100-dollar twin bed made of lightweight pine I never got around to painting are plenty good enough for a kid like me, right?

Kara summed it up well on the drive to Charlotte the day our IKEA trip finally arrived: "Because you're not married, you feel like you can't have nice things." I went on to vent about the frustration of buying yet another wedding gift, celebrating some twenty-two-years-olds' "passage into adulthood"—a place I had been residing for quite some time. Staying on as an employee at the divinity school where I earned my Master of Theological Studies degree several years ago—a program which prides itself on its young student body—means I have a constantly replenishing circle of young friends. My graduating class's weddings were just the beginning for me. As I age, the people around me stay the same, as I celebrate the same life transitions over and over again with new people; I tutor, teach, and mentor these young divinity students, and so become enmeshed in their lives. It comes as no surprise, then, that they wish to include me in these significant events.

I deposit my modest paycheck each month and wonder why, if I can't afford to buy myself new linens, I nonetheless feel obligated to buy them for someone else?

No one threw me a party when I graduated from college. No one paused to honor the day I signed my first lease and wrote the check for the first and last months' rent. Barely anyone even noticed when I handed in my master's thesis at Duke. I remember how I celebrated myself that day, having been urged by my therapist to do something, even if it was alone, even if it was small. I walked to my favorite bookstore and bought a mystery novel. Then I walked to the Indian buffet down the street and treated myself to a rare meal out before going home to settle in with the first real pleasure reading I'd enjoyed in a year.

It's not quite the same as a bridal shower, a bachelorette party, *and* a wedding, where everyone you know furnishes your kitchen, bathroom, *and* your lingerie drawer.

Still, that was actually a pretty nice way to celebrate for me, anticlimatic though it was. I enjoyed two of my favorite things, I paused to honor the moment I accomplished one of my life goals. I had arrived at a new place in life, which was thrilling but also terrifying. Within a week the terror of the job search would take over, and I knew that. It was good to be content with an achievement for a few moments, first.

Despite my many bitter rants about the state of my kitchen, my frustration doesn't stem from jealousy about the *stuff*, in the end (though I wouldn't complain if someone threw me an apartment warming party one of these days). It's about what all the stuff represents. The materials of the domestic sphere, the things you need now that you're a grown-up doing grown-up things. We mark selected, approved life transitions with material goods, and with big, expensive parties. The approved points on that path to grown-up land have not been present on my map. So, no parties. No registries. Just me and a mystery novel, curled up in my bed. My *twin* bed.

This past year I reached my limit at the wedding of a friend seven years younger than myself, a divinity school student I'd only gotten to know in the past year while helping her with her writing. Perhaps it was that I was one of only two single women at the wedding. Perhaps it was the fact that I house-sat for her while she was on her honeymoon, bringing in box after box that arrived from Amazon and Bed, Bath, & Beyond, wondering what wedding gifts were inside. I was done. More boxes arrived that week than could possibly have fit inside my own apartment. For my own well-being, I resolved that—with the exception of my best friend and my siblings—I would not be going to any more showers of any kind. I was sick of contributing to a way of life that congratulates people with kitchen appliances most of them will never use, of pretending I thought all of this made sense, that somehow by falling in love and getting married my friends deserved a new flat screen TV and a panini maker. That these events also continued make me feel inadequate by their very nature, when all the rest of the time I was reasonably satisfied with my life, made me all the more determined to quit playing the game.

The summer after this staunch resolution, after renewing the lease on my sweet little studio, I decided that I should admit after three years in the same apartment that I am quite settled, and that it would be okay to spend some of my hard-earned money on some furniture I actually liked. Some *new* furniture.

I started going through closets to prepare for the IKEA adventure, donating clothing I hadn't worn since college to Goodwill, and then I posted an ad on my neighborhood LISTSERV about my twin bed, hoping to sell it. I did, within twenty-four hours, to a family whose little girl was just graduating to a "big girl bed."

They said she wanted to paint it pink.

Cash in my pocket, along with my grown-up credit card and IKEA wish list, I psyched myself up for the road trip to Charlotte. I wandered the aisles with Kara, sitting on different thicknesses of mattresses, comparing upholstery colors, considering additional throw pillows. In the housewares section I bought a wine rack, with every intention of also buying a lot of wine to fill it with, despite the fact that no one would be throwing me a "stock the bar" party (the latest addition to the flurry of marriage-related spending). As we wandered on to another show room, I found new bedding, and then a chest of drawers just the right size to nest in one of my gable windows. Three years in the same apartment, and I only just acquired a chest of drawers in which to store my sweaters.

Candles, dishcloths, a heavy wood cutting board, an ice cream scoop. I went on and on. I had never bought so much *stuff* in my life, though compared to the amount of stuff considered normal in the United States it wasn't that much. Even with a couple of large pieces of furniture my total was around $700—not all that much when you consider it was the first time I had ever made an attempt to truly furnish my own home.

I don't want that much. A comfortable couch in a color I like that fits in my small space, a place to keep my clothes when I'm not wearing them, a rack to store wine for last-minute entertaining, an ice cream scoop. *An ice cream scoop*, for God's sake—I made it to the age of twenty-nine without an ice cream scoop?

Kara and I didn't eat lunch until after three o'clock that day. It was the longest shopping day of my life. We could have eaten at IKEA, but found the prospect too creepy. An Episcopal priest whose first career was as an aerospace engineer, Kara, is now working on her *second* PhD—in theology. Minds like Kara's, in my experience, have a low tolerance for manipulative advertising, and she refused to be subdued by the smell of Swedish meatballs wafting toward the check-out aisle. The "life improvement" messages playing over and over combined with the significant purchases we were making felt like maybe we were falling for something, buying into a simulated world we thought we had rejected. It was too much. I wanted to buy a futon, but I had not yet bought into the message.

After Kara dropped me and all of my new stuff off at home I put on some music and got out my tool box—tools I'd bought myself when I first moved to North Carolina six years before. I set to work assembling things, eventually moving to the stage of pushing my new furniture around to different corners until I figured out where I liked it, and then lighting a new vanilla scented candle, settling in on the new sofa with a book and a cup of tea. It felt like home. It had been my home for a long time, but this was different. I was treating the space like that was true, like it was my home, not some transient space I could pick up and leave without a look back. The cat jumped up next to me, kneading my thigh with her soft white paws, purring loudly, expressing her approval of the situation.

I can't do much to change the emphasis on expensive gift giving, and the selective honoring of achievements that leaves most actual work-related accomplishments out. I can't change the fact that people associate marriage with adulthood, and quality furniture with marriage. But at least I can treat myself like an adult, and my apartment like a home.

Pencil Skirts & Power Ties

A t the start of a new semester I had lunch with two of my colleagues, Diana and Celia, both experienced teaching assistants in the Divinity School at Duke University where I work. About to embark on my first semester as a TA in Church History, I asked my veteran friends to share their secrets. Our lunch was planned as an opportunity for me to pester them with questions and hopefully relieve some of my pre-semester jitters. I wanted to know what worked, what did not, and what lessons they had learned the hard way.

Most of our male colleagues do not often, to my knowledge at least, engage in such collaborative efforts. The competitive, isolating world of doctoral programs, Duke or elsewhere, is not always conducive to helping one another. I work as a tutor in the Center for Theological Writing in the Divinity School, so I stand a step or two outside of that circle, which is usually a good thing. This opportunity to take on a TA job usually reserved for doctoral students was intimidating, though, and caused me to pause and reflect on what sort of world I was stepping into. As I clamber my way up the ladder of academia toward teaching, one of the improvements I notice brought by the slowly growing number of women in theology, beyond the obvious equality and diversity, might well be that young women have often been taught to collaborate and cooperate and support one another. Perhaps our competitive male colleagues could learn a thing or two about that. Be that as it may, my more numerous male graduate student friends did not offer their mentorship, not even in a condescending, paternalistic way. I am grateful to be working in a divinity school in a day and age when, while women are few, there are enough of us to provide each other with support and solidarity.

I enjoyed a rich conversation over egg salad sandwiches and raspberry crunch bars from Twinnie's, the cafe in the engineering school where my friends and I like to gather to avoid our students or less supportive colleagues eavesdropping. I was beginning to feel more confident in my own intellectual resources after our lively discussion of classroom dynamics, grading, and other nuts and bolts, when the conversation turned to the dreaded "p" word: *professional*. Specifically, our final topic for the day was professional clothing. Now, professional dress might not fill everyone with dread, but it has always been a source of stress for me. Working at a nonprofit organization for the last few years, and as a writing tutor, I have been able to happily get by wearing purple Chuck Taylors, jeans, and sweaters to work most every day. This suits my lifestyle as a bicycle commuter, a person with a limited budget, and someone who values comfort more than keeping up appearances.

During the orientation session held for teaching assistants the week before, one well-known, stately male divinity school professor adored among students—let's call him Dr. X—had expressed very clearly that he tells his "gentlemen" to wear a jacket, and preferably a tie, on the days they are teaching. He paused dramatically before adding, "I would not presume to tell a woman how to dress." He left it at that.

One of our female professors had also spoken about the importance of our clothing choices during this session. Her expectation for TAs emphasized the importance of showing up for class looking "put together." I was unsure what to do with such vague instructions. I feel put together in sneakers and jeans, but I knew this was not what she meant. Diana and Celia offered advice on outfits that had worked for them, such as who sells skirts long enough that they didn't worry about showing "too much leg," and good websites for discounted work clothing, given that buying dress clothing on a teaching assistant's pay is difficult if not impossible.

They talked about the need to *look* like a teacher whether you felt like one or not, which made sense to me as I embarked on my first semester in a new role. Still, like our professors who did not seem know what "professional" dress in academia might mean for a woman, we had no easy answer.

A jacket, preferably a tie. It sounds so simple.

When I conjure up an image of "professor" in my mind I see my awkward college professors, dressed in khaki pants, button-down shirts, perhaps a wool or corduroy blazer with elbow patches. In fact, I have a photograph of myself from my senior year at Hope College, standing next to my favorite history professor, wearing a crisp green oxford shirt and a brown corduroy blazer. He is wearing a blue oxford shirt. We both have glasses. When this photo appeared on Facebook, which in 2006 was just catching on as a way of sharing photos, all of my college friends posted comments about the future professor, "mini me," and so forth. I was bound for graduate school, and dressing the part. It didn't occur to me then that I was gender-bending when I mimicked the uniform of the male teachers around me. At Hope I was insulated by the enthusiastic support of nearly every male professor I had studied with; I didn't know yet how much gender would matter, the higher I climbed in that academic ivory tower. They didn't seem to notice I was a woman, and truth be told, most of the time neither did I.

Six years later, it feels so much more complicated. No longer a big fish in the small pond of a Midwestern liberal arts college, I think more about power dynamics in the classroom than I ever wanted to. At Hope I always felt supported and encouraged as a young scholar, my gender perhaps acknowledged but certainly not emphasized. I was taken seriously. At Duke, I know that as a 5'1" woman in a classroom composed primarily of young men I will be expected to prove myself in ways that Dr. X, with his deep voice and clerical collar, will not. Unlike my undergraduate history professor, who at some point let me start calling him Marc, at Duke the lines are clearly drawn between faculty and student. I stand in the nebulous place between.

Add to this the aversion I have felt toward fashion for much of my life, and cue a shopping-induced emotional meltdown.

There were so many questions to ask. Slacks or skirt? If a skirt, how short is too short and thus appears too sexy? How long is too long and thus appears matronly? If pants, well, women's bodies come in many shapes and sizes, so that may result in just as many questions of cut and style and length and where they sit on one's hips. And do you wear heels with them? How high? Do you want to risk stumbling in front of your students? Then again, would a little extra height add to the image of authority?

When it comes to blouses—mind you, men get shirts, women get "blouses"—there are very few ways around revealing the feminine form. Any top tailored enough to fit well—if you can find a button-down that neither gapes nor billows—will reveal that yes, in fact, you are a woman, and have breasts. Surprise! This is fine, my feminist conscience says. I don't flaunt my body, but neither should I feel the need to make it more masculine in the classroom. Yet in a world where women's bodies are constantly sexualized I know there are risks I don't want to take in class. So perhaps I should err on the side of dowdy, I tell myself. Or masculine. The problem is that if I show up for class in an ill-fitting oxford shirt and pants that are a bit too long, topped off with a blazer whose overly broad shoulders makes it feel like it was made for one of my male colleagues, instead of feeling professional and confident I feel like a little girl playing dress-up.

Instead of instilling me with confidence, "professional" garb makes me feel like a fraud. Deep down, this was the problem I was grappling with as I prepared to run a classroom for the first time. I was waiting to be found out—discovered as an underqualified wannabe. Not only was I expected to spend money I did not have on "professional" clothing no one can actually describe to me, I was worried that halfway through the semester I would be selling it all at a consignment shop because I had failed. I can't even figure out what to wear to class the first day. What can I teach students about church history?

If I were a man would it all be easier? The jacket, the tie. But also owning my place in the theological academy. I know that all young scholars experience this to some extent. I have dear friends, many of them men, who have echoed my sentiments at times. The imposter complex. We are all trying to establish ourselves, and I know this is hard for them, too. Yet the challenges I hear from the women around me, the struggles inside my own head, are different. Teaching about the history of the church, which has not been kind to women, which has not affirmed their personhood, their teaching abilities, their intellect, their voices—teaching about that church, as a woman, is hard in ways that go beyond the intellectual issues. The real possibility that I will have students in my class who don't believe in women's ordination is doubly so.

I worry about whether I know enough to teach. I worry because of my own spiritual struggles to make sense of the church, and of my place in it. Dr. X and his "I would not presume . . ." statement speak far beyond dress. When he says those words, what I hear is, "I'm not quite sure what to *do* with all you women folks." If he and his colleagues can ignore that we are women, that we are in fact different than men, both biologically and in terms of our ways of living into—or not—socially constructed gender norms, then he is okay. He affirms our call to serve the church, to preach and to teach. Yet if he is forced to consider our differences—in dress, in body, in voice—and the difference our inclusion makes, he is at a loss.

That is how the church feels to me, sometimes. It is how the academy feels, too. As long as your femininity isn't showing everything moves along swimmingly, but if you reveal too much you will get into trouble.

I have never been a girly-girl, so I can play along at first. My tendency to mimic men's academic clothing in college has continued, though I have developed my own style over the years. I wear earrings more than I used to, and have developed a fondness for colorful scarves, both accessories adding a feminine touch to my T-shirt–and–jeans uniform without being as overt as short skirts or silk blouses. I have never been much for revealing clothing.

Thus, I can blend in with the boys and still look "put together." Still, I am naturally quiet, shy, introverted. I am highly sensitive. My voice is higher, and softer, than my male colleagues. I am short and curvy. You can only ignore my feminine form for so long before it stares you in the face, and if you still ignore it I will probably bring it front and center with a question about how the topic we are discussing looks from a feminist angle.

I think Dr. X would prefer that we be more like Macrina, sister of Saint Gregory of Nyssa, known for her devotion to the church as a nun after the death of her fiancé. In Church History class he puts her on a pedestal when we read Nyssa's description of her devotion and death, which details how she eschews feminine ways. She is supposed to show how we might all transcend gender and interact with one another beyond such confines. The problem is that Macrina did not so much transcend gender, in her brother's narrative, as she did perform male roles—thus rendering herself more fully human, in my professor's eyes. Again and again Nyssa describes how Macrina was "like a man," as he lauds her spiritual accomplishments. Transcending gender in the early church meant transcending femaleness. Men already possess that particular virtue by birth.

Jacket and tie. Virtue and virility—from the same Latin root, *virtus*. Meaning courage, excellence, character, *manliness*.

If I dress up in a pencil skirt of the perfect length, a blouse that fits just so, heels that give me some extra height without setting me off balance, then will I have performed correctly? Or, if I opt for trousers, a tweed blazer, and a bow tie, then will I have it right?

After a hellish day at the outlet mall, where I bought a sweater, a chambray shirt, two new pairs of earrings, and tried on tons of slacks and skirts and blouses and blazers—none of which fit me—I decided that I refuse to follow someone else's rules about how I should dress when teaching. Thankfully, the professor I am working with told me she has "no sartorial rules" for her teaching assistants, anyway. Dr. X has no say in my dress, so it is just as well he would not "presume" to give me instructions.

As I got ready for bed the night before class began, I thought about the two-page outline I'd written out for the next day's discussion on martyrdom in the early church. I was well prepared. My students were mostly in their early twenties, fresh out of college, all in their first semester of graduate school, and according to their answers the incoming student survey, they were mostly terrified. I felt confident in my knowledge, and ready for this next step, though my stomach was also in knots. First day nerves were inevitable, I told myself. Knowing the students were nervous helped me think of my role as one in which I could also be accessible, approachable, helpful—a source of calm in what will be a difficult semester for many of them. The question I was asking was not "How do I perform the role of *teacher* the way Dr. X says I should?" It was, "What kind of teacher do I want to be?"

I want to be a teacher who you can call by her first name. I want students to feel as comfortable asking me to explain the finer points of the early church councils as they do bursting into tears because they don't know what they got themselves into when they decided to go to divinity school. I want to be a teacher who doesn't need to change the way I dress in order to be taken seriously.

So, as I picked out my clothing for the first day, I picked things I liked, and things I felt comfortable in. I thought fondly of my friend Sueli, who was the Portuguese translator on a study trip I took in Brazil when I was in divinity school myself years before, who told me that in Brazil jeans were appropriate for everything. I have embraced her approach to denim ever since, and on this occasion I lay my favorite indigo-washed skinny jeans across the chair by my bed for the next day. I contemplated my shirt options. Blue striped oxford? Black blazer? No, it was too hot for that. That flowing, lightweight, sleeveless silk top would be perfect for late August in North Carolina, though. I laid it on top of the jeans. Now, to choose some shoes. After stressing out about clothing for the last few weeks, laughing with some male friends about what they call the "first week of school power tie," I came to this conclusion: high heels are the female equivalent of a tie. In my days as a wedding assistant at Duke Chapel while I was a student I had learned to walk confidently in heels in spite of myself, though I refuse anything taller than two inches and consider stilettos torture devices for women's feet designed with the triumph of the patriarchy in mind. I have one pair of camel colored peep-toe pumps that would almost qualify as comfortable. I now call them my power shoes. They are my one concession to playing the "professional" game, one that I can affirm because it subtly undermines it at the same time. My friend Joelle says they are sexy shoes, and while I have never understood how shoes can be sexy, there is something empowering about choosing to wear decidedly feminine shoes in a masculine setting. My feet aren't sexy, but you sure aren't going to see Dr. X in shoes like these.

When I walked into class the next morning I wasn't thinking about my clothes, though. I felt comfortable, I felt like myself, I felt ready (or at least, as ready as I was ever going to be). In an ill-fitting suit or a pencil skirt, any of the things suggested to me by others in the previous weeks, I would have felt fake, and I would have been preoccupied with wondering whether I was doing things "right"— whether I was doing things the way the theological big boys do. But if they need me to wear a suit in order to take me seriously, they have issues to work through that are no concern of mine.

Personally, I think martyrdom, eschatology, and the christological controversies are so much more interesting than any dress code could ever be. My outfit may or may not qualify as "put together," but my lecture notes are.

Performance

I set my heavy messenger bag down at the table across from Sarah. It was an unseasonably warm evening in November, and she had already snagged a table outside at Cocoa Cinnamon, our favorite coffee shop in Durham, where she is a graduate student at Duke Divinity School. Working as a tutor in the writing center there since graduating myself, I enjoy getting to know students like Sarah, and the lively conversations about theology, feminism, and politics that inevitably transpire when we get together. My own graduate school classmates have mostly moved away, and the ever-replenishing student body meets my need for interesting conversation partners. This is one reason I keep my job at Duke despite the risk of being seen as one of those people who just never moved on after graduating. Tonight Sarah is working on a project for a women's studies course she's taking. I have a stack of essays to comment on for students I am meeting with tomorrow.

As we struggled to focus on our work instead of jabbering on about other things, as we are wont to do, Sarah looks up, sighs admiringly, and interjects, "God, you have great hair."

"Thanks." My only response. I have learned not to say more, lest we end up talking about my hair for ten minutes.

"It's so sexy," she continues.

I sigh. "Oh. Yes, I guess. Did I ever tell you that in college I wore it really short and spiky? I miss that sometimes."

"NO." Sarah stared. "Never do that again."

Now it was my turn to stare. Here was one of the smartest women I know, a self-identified feminist, and budding theology scholar, and her intonation seemed to be suggesting that it would be a tragedy to cut my hair.

Sarah herself has hair as long as mine, chestnut brown, shiny and healthy, that curls perfectly and compliments her bright blue eyes. Sarah is beautiful. So beautiful that, insecure as I was in college, I would have assumed in the past that we could never be friends. She wears bright pink lipstick to class, gutsy and gorgeous, defying the boring tweed uniform of the academy.

I shrugged it off, and we went back to our conversation, but later I found myself daydreaming about cutting all of my hair off again. While it felt good to be admired, to be complimented, it also felt frustratingly reductive. Something about the horror in Sarah's voice, that shocked stare, made me sad. Maybe it was that she seemed so unaware of her own beauty. Maybe it was that she projected such a limited understanding of mine.

"A woman with a good haircut can make a trash bag look stylish." These words of wisdom, from my mother, were relayed to me when I was maybe twelve or thirteen. Though to look at her you would never peg her as a style snob of any kind, I blame my mom for my unwillingness to settle for Great Clips or Haircuts Plus. She has worn her own hair in a short, practical way for most of my life, and my affinity for jeans and soft cotton T-shirts can likely be traced to her influence. I rarely wear make-up, I avoid buying new clothing, and I only learned when I moved south from Michigan to North Carolina after my college graduation that some people consider a mani-pedi part of the ordinary upkeep of femininity rather than a luxury. But when it comes to my hair I will gladly drop fifty dollars or more for a simple cut and blowout from a skilled stylist. This is not vanity so much as a tangled history of love and hate between my hair and myself.

My parents both had hair down to their waists when they married in the 70s, hippies then, though they have long since been domesticated by their four children and the church. Not long after my birth my dad finished his associates degree (I was even present for his graduation, I'm told) and began work as a custodian at what was then the Upjohn Company, though Pfizer has since taken them over, soon working his way into a position as an HVAC, which is what he went to school for. My mom went back to her administrative job at the hospital after I was born, but within weeks she decided to stay home with my older sister Heidi and me full-time. Eventually they made friends with some folks in an evangelical bible study group called the Navigators, became "born-again" Christians, and had two more babies—my sister Holly, and the youngest, my brother Andrew. They home schooled all four of us, kindergarten through twelfth grade, sending us on to colleges and graduate schools they never would have dreamed of attending themselves.

At home last summer for my older sister Heidi's wedding, I flipped through a family photo album, looking at pictures from their wedding for the first time since childhood, wondering where these free-spirited people had gone. My mother wore a simple ivory dress that would have suited a wedding in a meadow better than their family-only Catholic mass, but I thought she looked radiant, her cheeks flushed with joy, that wide smile so familiar, so like the one I see in the mirror each morning.

"You look beautiful in these pictures, Mom," I said. "I can't believe I'd forgotten these."

She told me how she woke up that morning, braided my dad's hair, and pinned the veil on her own head. Meanwhile, today we were all carefully crafting our appearance for Heidi and my soon-to-be brother-in-law Eric's wedding, which looked like a circus compared with that of my parents, though it was tame and tasteful by contemporary standards. Heidi had chosen the most sought-after location in our hometown for her reception, the historic Rose Street Market, and the ceremony itself would happen in the picturesque chapel at Kalamazoo College, where Heidi and Eric met. Friends were flying in from all over the country. Over the past year and a half each detail of this day had been meticulously planned, and we would be celebrating late into the night.

The idea of my mother braiding my father's hair and donning that simple white veil was a telling juxtaposition to Heidi, in front of her make-up mirror, gluing on false eyelashes and painting her face. More like my mother in this respect, I still turn to Heidi whenever I am at a loss about proper attire for formal occasions, and this week had been no exception. From the sweet pink high heeled shoes I would wear later in the afternoon on up to the pearls around my neck and the luscious salon-styled curls carefully pinned back from my face, today I was a product of Heidi's fashion intelligence, her artistic eye. Still, I must admit, I felt a bit like a gorilla in a tutu.

Returning to the photo album, I considered my father's image, standing next to my mom in her flower child dress, wearing a grey suit and a ruffled pink shirt. My favorite photos are the ones from behind, where you can see that long braid of hair hanging down his back—hair that looks a lot like mine, today. These days they both have short hair, my mother's mostly grey, though she had it colored in preparation for the wedding, a way of soothing her nerves about being the center of attention when she is escorted to her seat at the beginning of the service today. My father's hair is as thick as ever, though he too is starting to go grey. Months from now there will be another photo to put alongside their wedding photos—dad in a contemporary black tux, mom in a cornflower blue mother-of-the-bride dress and earrings she borrowed from me, my one unique style contribution. The smiles are unchanged.

In childhood pictures from seven or eight years after my parents' wedding I am chubby and blond, my hair in two pigtails on either side of my head, usually clutching my teddy bear and blanket in one arm, thumb stuck in my mouth. My hair turned darker as I grew older, to match the light brown of my parents'— someone once described it as the color of straw—and when I was old enough to have an opinion about how it was cut, I wore it in a chin length bob. This was my style for years.

The winter after I turned fifteen I was obsessed with figure skating. My coach, Lisa, was a student at the local university whose rink I practiced in—she was sophisticated and smart, and wore her blonde hair in a pixie cut, the kind that is coming back into style now, more than a decade later. I wanted to be just like Lisa. I got the name of her stylist, and made an appointment.

The stylist clipped and snipped and buzzed, and sent me home. The result was not a younger looking version of my coach. My hair looked fine—in hindsight, I think it looked good—but it was not what I had wanted. My hair—my thick, straight, voluminous hair—grows directly away from my scalp, like a chia pet. Those volume producing shampoos people waste money on? I have never needed those. My friend Hunter put it best, perhaps, asking me for advice a few weeks later.

"How do you get your hair to stand up like that?"

My answer was, nothing. I spent my time trying to get it to lay down.

As a fifteen-year-old girl with short hair, I did not feel much like the pixie short haircuts are named after.

The short hair was not the only problem, though, or even the main one. My hair was never what I wanted it to be in all those years of chin length bobs, either. I did not try anything new until high school because I figured it was doomed to failure. I continued to struggle with my hair, trying to get it to lay down flat, wondering whether anything could make it closer to some definition of "cute" I had adopted from the images of tall, skinny girls with neatly coiffed blonde locks in the pages of *Seventeen Magazine*, but even if I had managed it, what then? Would I have been satisfied? In any case, I was neither tall nor particularly skinny. Hair was easier to manipulate than my other body worries, so I asked Heidi to help me put blonde highlights in it in hopes that would get me closer to the image in my head, a version of me that would match that of the magazines' glossy pages. My hair turned orange, though, and my mom made me pay for the professional highlights I got to cover the damage out of my own pocket money, saved from weekends working at the local ice rink, where I rented skates to wannabe hockey players and twirling children for four dollars an hour. The college guys I worked with said they liked my new hairstyle, but

I always assumed it was one of their all-too-common attempts to embarrass the only high school girl on staff by flirting. It worked.

Later that year, in addition to my individual coaching in ice dancing and freestyle skating, I joined a synchronized skating team. We traveled around the state for competitions, and when we performed we were all expected to wear our hair the same way—twenty girls in purple velvet and lace, gliding, lunging, turning in unison, our hair pulled tightly into matching buns.

I did not have enough hair for a bun. So, I bought a fake one.

Before competitions I would sit in a hotel room while the team mom would slick my short hair down with a half a bottle of cheap blue hair gel, and go to work with a box of bobby pins, attaching that puffy brown donut of plastic hair to the back of my head. It was mortifying, but the hair piece was surprisingly convincing.

I quit the team my senior year of high school, though, and within a week I walked into the salon again, embraced my hair's desire to stand on end, and went shorter than ever. My classmates barely recognized me the next day. It was liberating at the time to cut off all that hair after fighting with it for so long. Enough of the flyaways, the split ends, wishing it was something other than it was. I could just cut it off. I could make it go away.

In college, though, the regular haircuts were too expensive, so I let it grow long again. By the time I was a senior it was everywhere: in my face at the gym, in the sink drain, on the back of my black cardigan making me look more frumpy than I already was from those latte-fueled late nights in the library in the days when I might only eat a protein bar for lunch so that I did not have to take a break from my work. I wore my hair in a ponytail nearly every day that year. Secretly, I still wished it was thinner or flatter or curlier, lighter or darker, red or blonde or even pink. Anything but what it was, this unmanageable, boring mop, an unkempt mess of straw-colored something that I never knew how to style.

This insecurity about not just my hair, but my looks in general, had been an issue for me throughout college, highlighted by the comparisons that living in an all-women's dorm inevitably prompted. Instead of acknowledging that, I focused on my studies. I pretended to be above such concerns, rolling my eyes at conversations about fashion in the cafeteria, skipping out on movie night in the residence hall, when the other women would inevitably watch yet another romantic comedy. I genuinely believed I had more important things to worry about, though in truth my other concerns also became a way of ignoring deeper insecurities I did not want to acknowledge or work through. I was thinking about Dante, Austen, Nietzsche, and Kierkegaard. I was focused on my job as an RA, on ultimate frisbee practice, and how to tell my parents that I wanted to change my major to philosophy. The ponytail, the practical clothing I chose, the reluctance to wear make-up—this was my own aesthetic allegiance, no less thought out than that of the sorority girls in my classes who wore designer jeans and high heels with the hoodie sweatshirts that proudly proclaimed their Greek affiliation. I cared about looking like I didn't care.

At some point, well into my twenties, my college days behind me, this distaste for my own hair, and the insecurities I felt more generally, began to bother me. More so, what bugged me was the way every woman I knew exhibited similar feelings. Women with straight hair try to curl it. Women with curly hair spend hours with a straightener—and more hours trying to repair the damage done to their hair by heat styling, using expensive products that, most likely, do nothing. Nothing, except perhaps poison us with creepy chemicals that seep into our skin, messing with our fertility and probably giving us cancer. We cut, dye, let grow, condition, cut again, highlight, lowlight, blow out, up-do. We mess with our hair. We complain about our hair. Do we, ever, love—or even like—our hair?

As an overly intellectual graduate student, I became increasingly frustrated by the sense that we want any hair except the hair we were born with, and so I became my own experiment. I would let my hair grow. Let it grow until I could almost sit on it. I would make myself take good care of it, and I thought that maybe I could learn to like it. Or to be content with it. Or, once and for all, to really not care. I wanted to make peace with my hair.

This was a kind of ridiculous endeavor, the kind that perhaps only an overly enthusiastic graduate student would undertake.

There were a few hiccups along the way. First, since as mentioned my hair is really thick, it takes a long time to wash. And a lot of shampoo. Low-maintenance Meghan was not amused by these factors. So I started skipping days. First, I washed my hair every other day. That middle day drove me nuts for months, until I stopped noticing it because my hair just didn't need to be washed as often anymore. I started skipping another day. Eventually, I skipped another. Suddenly I felt like I was back on the backpacking trip I took my senior year of college when I didn't wash my hair for a whole week. I read articles in fashion magazines that explained why my previous daily wash habit was actually bad for my hair, and the best part of my new knowledge was I was able to pay less attention to my hair than ever.

There were other changes, too. I bought a curling iron, which I even used a handful of times. During the winter I couldn't let my hair air dry anymore for fear of catching cold by going outdoors with such a heavy wet mass hanging from my head on chilly mornings, so on wash days I would blow it dry slowly with a boar bristle brush, and learned how it was that a person could get her hair to actually *shine*. When babysitting for my friend's kids, I'd let them play salon, brushing and braiding my hair while I sat cross-legged on the living room floor. Over the summer I sat outside and let it air dry in the North Carolina heat, and natural highlights started to appear. Long hair became a part of my routine, and I learned ways to keep that from making my life more complicated. Good hair, I found, didn't have to mean excessive fixation on my appearance every day.

In contrast, other people started commenting on my hair all the time. How healthy it looked, how thick it is, what a lovely color. I was shocked. People had never talked about my hair this much before—not even when it was shockingly short—and now it was the first thing they noticed. Sometimes it felt like it was the only thing they noticed.

I was learning that I have great hair. I was also learning that this is really annoying sometimes. Suddenly my hair became this central part of my identity in a way it never had been, not even when I cut it short, which ought to have been so much more of a dramatic, rebellious act than wearing it long. Long hair is so *ordinary*. I was performing my femininity in a way I had never wanted to, in a way that my decision to let my hair grow long had never been intended to serve. My plan was not to become more feminine; my plan was to challenge the notion that femininity necessitated discontentment with my physical appearance. Would I ever learn that life and my theories do not always fit so neatly together?

Though I've thought about it several times, I still have not cut off all my hair again, because despite everything I guess my plan succeeded. I rather like my hair, and I think I will keep it around for a while. I do not want curly hair or red hair or blonde hair anymore (though pink still strikes me as a fun possibility). I want my hair.

But I absolutely do not want my hair to be the first thing anyone notices about me, to be reduced to these flowing locks, however beautiful they may be. I do not want people to gasp when I suggest cutting them off again. I certainly reject the assertion that my short hair would be any less sexy. I will continue to wear my hair however I damn well please.

Last Saturday I took my time blowing my hair dry, picking out a clean, comfortable, plain white v-neck tee, pulling on my favorite skinny jeans. I even put on mascara before donning my thick black glasses, tying my purple converse sneakers, and grabbing my leather jacket. I was going dancing.

My friend Graham throws a big house party every couple months or so, transforming his living room into a dance floor by moving all of the furniture out, save a table in a corner that transforms into a makeshift DJ booth. I met Graham, and a handful of other students who would be at this party, through a mutual friend in the same graduate program with him at the University of North Carolina. As I biked over to his house, a couple miles from mine,

I laughed at memories of my own graduate school days—no one ever danced at our parties. Our parties were, simply put, *lame* (everything you'd expect from a bunch of nerdy graduate students). I was still getting used to hanging around with this new group of graduate students who knew how to have a good time doing something other than talking about school. I liked it.

All of my usual wingmen had other plans this weekend, but I wasn't about to let the lack of a friend-date keep me home. I wanted to dance in the freedom of a loud, crowded, sweaty room. I always dance by myself, or maybe in a group, rather than with anyone in particular, and my male friends are used to serving as my bodyguard in case of creeps in clubs. Anyway, going places alone is the norm for me these days, and I've settled into it such that making an entrance at a party on my own no longer makes me want to sink into the floor. I've learned how to carry myself, I suppose. To play the part of confident, sexy, single girl, maybe even to own it, on occasion.

When I first arrived there was no one else around I knew yet; there was a basketball game tonight, so the student crowd had not begun to trickle in. Graham was busy in the corner with his headphones and laptop, doing whatever it is that contemporary DJs do. I poured myself a drink and chatted with a biology graduate student in the kitchen until I heard Micah yell at me from across the room, "MEGHAN, WHY AREN'T YOU DANCING?"

One of my newer acquaintances, Micah is flamboyant, enthusiastic, fun. Everything I wasn't when I was twenty-three, as he is now. I finished my drink, and made my way to the dance floor, but by the time I arrived Micah had stepped out for a cigarette. (Kids these days. They missed the barrage of no smoking ads I grew up with, maybe, or perhaps they simply choose to ignore them.) The dance floor was filled with people I didn't know, and I calculated my next move. Dance alone? Join Micah in the cold, and resist bumming a smoke?

A young man in a white button-down with black glasses said, "Hello!" I turned around, startled, and said hi. I'd never seen him before. I decided this was sufficient invitation to join the circle of strangers.

As I moved toward the center of the crowd, where I tend to be most comfortable, the man in the glasses shifted around behind me, moving his body closer to mine. I ignored this, as I continued dancing on my own. On the next song he moved closer still, and I felt his hand tentatively brush my waist. I shifted away ever so slightly, not so much uncomfortable as surprised. Surprised that I would catch a man's eye at a party the minute I entered the room. Surprised, maybe, that I kind of felt like dancing with him, that my defenses were down. Then there was small detail of my crush on the DJ, an unrealistic fantasy I was trying to get over. I caught myself wondering whether dancing with this man would catch Graham's eye; serious graduate student that he is, that seemed difficult to imagine, even on Saturday night, especially at his own party. His mind was elsewhere. It was always elsewhere.

I danced on in this awkward, noncommittal way—not pushing the glasses man away, but not quite dancing with him, either. I got thirsty, and while I was in the kitchen getting water the man from the dance floor approached me.

"I don't want to be all high school about this, but I'm going to anyway. I'd like to dance with you more; is that okay?"

It was an awkward introduction, but I heard myself saying, "Sure." Now I really did feel like I was in high school, but his manners—and request for consent—were refreshing. I introduced myself. He said his name was Chris.

As the night wore on I relaxed into the music. My earlier embarrassment faded easily, quickly. I liked the way I felt, my body moving with another person's body, the music moving through us. His hands wandered, held me close, and I felt sexy. I felt desired. I didn't think about Graham, and I didn't think about whether he was thinking about me, either, until later when, after giving Chris my phone number, a thing I almost never do, he asked if he could kiss me. Graham was standing two feet from me, and I did not know what I wanted. I smiled a calculated shy smile, and tapped my cheek with one finger, an invitation to a subtler action.

We danced. Sweating and swaying in unison. I felt his hands on both my hips, pressing into my warm flesh, and I had no desire to move away. Though I usually prefer to dance alone, I do understand why people liked to dance with other people. Tonight, it felt good. His hands traced my body, coming to rest on my hair.

My hair. Chris ran his fingers through my hair and I pulled away ever so slightly, without thinking.

I wasn't worried he would mess it up; it is long and straight and does what it does. There's nothing one could do to mess it up. Low-maintenance Meghan is still low maintenance.

This man's hands were traveling around my body a moment ago; I had nearly let him kiss me. Yet when I felt his fingers in my hair, did that cross some invisible line? It was all fun and games, dancing. But touching my hair was an intimacy reserved for someone else.

My hair is part of me. Touching it, running your fingers through it—this is a sensory experience both playful and sensual. My hair *is* sexy, as Sarah so often reminds me. And I felt sexy on the dance floor that night. But a stranger's fingers felt out of place running through my hair. It felt like cheating, somehow. Like I was cheating myself out of the real intimacy I wanted, ultimately, by letting this man I didn't know revel in my gorgeous hair.

I took his hands in mine, guided them back to my waist. He left soon after that, but I danced until the music stopped at 2 AM. Graham worried that it was too late for me to bike home, though I insisted it wasn't; he loaded my bike in the back of his beat-up Camry, and drove me himself. In my driveway we said good night, and hugged like friends—or, maybe, friends who could be something else if they tried.

Closing the door behind me that night, I wondered if Chris would call. I wondered if I wanted him to. I wondered how it would feel to let Graham run his hands through my hair.

Hers

I met Mia when she was three months old. A mutual friend put me in touch with Carla and Lindsey, Mia's parents, after learning they were searching for a childcare provider. Carla—a minister—was preparing to return to her job at a local church. I had recently graduated from divinity school myself, and was struggling to find meaningful work. Or any work.

Lindsey often introduces me as Mia's "third mom." In hindsight it might have been awkward the first time she assigned me such a significant title, when she named me as part of what might already look like an atypical family to some. Mia is almost four, and I have been taking care of her since she was a wee infant, laying helpless on blanket, smiling and cooing and crying and cooing some more. Our days together followed a predictable rhythm: eat, play, poop, nap, repeat. Sometimes we walked in the park, or sat on a blanket spread out on the front porch with her set in the middle, rocking back and forth contentedly while I read her Sandra Boynton board books and worked on my tan. Until she started preschool, the only people she spent more time with than me were her actual parents, so the title "third mom" seems appropriate. I grew into it.

One of the things my friends who work as nannies have struggled with, though, is boundaries—and jealousy. If you are doing childcare full-time—which I was for quite a while, having graduated in 2009, which was arguably one of the worst years to finish a degree in basically anything, especially the humanities—you will become really close with those children. If you let yourself, or maybe even if you try not to let yourself, you might come to love them. Scarier still, they might love you back. This creates the potential for both joy and jealousy, a reality my fellow nannies, babysitters, childcare providers—whatever you call us—have experienced firsthand.

My friends' stories made me paranoid that at some point Carla and Lindsey might be upset about the affection I shared with their child. My connection to Mia was a reality early on. I worried about her parents resenting me and the obvious closeness that developed between us. Perhaps it was silly of me, though. I remember Carla telling me, after her first week back at work, my second week on the job (since I had spent the first week with both Carla and Mia so that everyone could get acquainted) that people kept asking her if she was nervous about leaving Mia, if it was hard, if she felt distracted. She said no.

"I just feel like you and Mia have this bond already. I don't know what it is, but somehow it leaves me at ease."

At that point I was anything but "at ease." Mia was the first infant I had been in charge of for significant periods of time. I spent the previous six years, since I graduated from high school, avoiding babysitting as much as possible. I had never before been a "baby person." I had never understood young women who burst into excited baby talk the moment a baby entered a room. (I still don't, baby lover though I may be.) I felt like I had no idea what I was doing, and I still could not believe Carla and Lindsey had hired me. What if the baby started crying and wouldn't stop? What if she choked on something? What if—what if—what IF . . .

Of course, when I held Mia during my informal interview with Carla and Lindsay she cried the whole time. It was bedtime, but at the time it felt personal. I had gone home that night feeling sure I would be back to applying for jobs the next day. Maybe Carla and Lindsey saw something in me I never knew was there; I am certainly grateful they gave me the space for that to grow.

I became a nanny, and for months I was full of those "what ifs," with new ones added almost daily. The biggest was, "What

if this is all I'm good for?" What if "nanny" was the only thing I
was qualified for, what if I never got a better job, what if I went to
school for nothing and the bottom line was that as a woman all
anyone wanted me for was childcare?

I was really depressed that year. Most days I felt useless, stupid, like a total failure. I settled into the routine of caring for Mia,
but tried to treat my work as a nanny like any other job. "A job
is just a job," I said to myself, again and again. My work did not
define me. I was still smart, capable, successful.

One afternoon, a few months into my work as a nanny, when
I heard some noises coming from Mia's nursery, I cracked the door
and tiptoed in. She was awake. I turned on the lights, revealing
her fuzzy black curls and endless brown eyes, and she smiled up at
me, her tiny arms reaching out, happy to see me. Happy to see *me*.
Happy to see *me*.

My job is to love you, I thought. What I said was, "Good
morning, Mia! How was your nap?" I felt like I might burst into
tears, like something was growing in my chest, the roots of some
strange new plant intertwining with my organs, squeezing them in
a way that was painful but that I somehow hoped would never go
away. Perhaps Mia's tiny hand had reached inside and taken hold
of me, and instead of hurt or fear or confinement it felt like I had a
reason to get up in the morning. Like maybe I mattered, somehow,
to this tiny person who did not even know how to talk yet. I picked
her up.

"I love you Mia." There was no response, of course. I fed her a
bottle, and later when Carla got home I waved goodbye. She lifted
her tiny fist in my direction.

There was no miraculous change in our day-to-day activities
just because I loved her. I continued to wonder what I was doing with my life. I read intense volumes of theology and critical
theory during her naps—I think that was the year my mind was
a mash-up of Dietrich Bonhoeffer and Judith Butler. I applied for
jobs all over the country that I had little actual interest in. I tried to
write when I could summon the emotional wherewithal, and understood for the first time how much mental space I really needed

in order to write, but also how to deal with what I had—a twenty-minute nap, sometimes, or on good days as much as two hours. Fall turned to winter, then spring, and eventually the trees began to bloom, pollen filled the air, and tiny green inchworms dropped into Mia's pink, orange, and brown–striped umbrella stroller on our daily walks. Mia was getting used to eating solid foods by this time, and I sat in front of her, spooning mashed avocado—her favorite—into her smiling mouth with a tiny spoon. Sometimes mealtimes seemed like more of a game to her than anything else. I looked down at the bowl for a moment, and when I lifted my eyes again the avocado I thought she had already swallowed splattered all over my face and shirt.

I burst into tears.

"Mia, I love you, but what am I doing?" I wailed. "I have a master's degree, in theology, from DUKE." For months I had denied my disappointment in myself. I hated the idea that my life might look like a failure to anyone else, so I pretended to be content. I was studying for the GRE and applying to PhD programs. This was all part of the grand ten-year plan.

That day, I just cried. I realized how ridiculous it was to say any of those things to a baby, of course, but then one of my strengths as a nanny was speaking to Mia a lot, reading to her constantly, trying to teach her letters and numbers and colors long before she could say anything back to me. I would like to take at least partial credit for her young brilliance today.

I pulled myself together, grabbed a rag, wiped up the avocado. There was nothing else I could do.

There were hundreds of days like that. Playing, reading, feeding. Diapers and bottles. Learning to walk. Eventually learning to talk. Sometime later I stood in the kitchen with both Carla and Lindsey, a rare occasion when all of us were there at the same time. Mia had been verbalizing variations of "mama" and "mommy" for a while now, toddling around, developing her own personality. She clung to Mama Carla's leg, and looked over at me.

"Geg-en," she said.

Lindsey squealed, Carla laughed, and I just stood there. *She said my name.*

Lindsey looked at Carla, and at me. "Am I the only one whose heart is beating fast?"

I have no idea what I said. I suppose I didn't know what to say. The combined emotions set off by this child I loved so dearly saying my *name*, and the fact that her parents were as joyful as I—heck, the fact that I cared about a child mumbling something that no one but we three would even identify as a word—well, it was too much for words just then.

I remember when I decided to go back to school, how Carla and Lindsey would check in on how the applications were going, on whether or not I had heard back from any schools. How I would sit and talk with them over dinner, after work, like part of the family, as they debated what to do if I got into graduate school again, if I moved, if my days taking care of Mia came to an end. We'd talk about Carla's search for a job as a senior pastor, about her ministry, and my work started to feel like ministry, too. I made it possible for Carla to do good work by doing this good work of caring for her daughter.

We sat around that table together a lot. We laughed at the funny things Mia did, at our failed attempts to cope with temper tantrums in the park, at the silly things she said, at the ways she surprised us each day. We cried together about the ongoing challenges for Carla and Lindsey as a same-sex couple in North Carolina, where an anti-marriage amendment had recently passed. We all wondered in different ways about what will come next. Mia was what brought us together most though, I think. Mia, and our love for her.

I remember, too, those days when one of them would come home from work and Mia would be sad that I was leaving. We had conversations about how I lived somewhere else, but that I would come back. I would always come back. She could come see me too, could come stay at my apartment. She struggled with the word—apartment. A lot of syllables for her mouth to shape.

Mia is in school now, and so am I. I come over for dinner every Tuesday. Mia likes to play hostess, and make sure I have a glass of water and a place at the table that usually hosts just their family of three. She likes to ask me when I am going to Charlotte again, for another writing residency. Charlotte is where her Nana and Papa live. She asks if I will see Chance, their dog, while I'm there. In turn, I ask her what she is learning in preschool. She tells me about musical instruments, about insects and their exoskeletons, sings her ABCs, tells me the names of her friends. They have a tire swing at her school. That is her favorite.

A couple of weeks ago, Carla and Lindsey invited a new baby-sitter over to meet Mia, since I have been short on time even for weekend date nights lately, what with being a student and working several jobs. After the potential sitter left, Carla asked Mia how she felt about their new friend taking care of her sometime so that Mama and Mommy could go out.

"I want Meghan."

"Meghan isn't going away, Mia," Carla said. "But sometimes Meghan has plans too, so she can't always take care of you when Mama and Mommy go places."

"I want Meghan."

We laughed together about this over dinner the following Tuesday when Carla told me. The cute moment cuts deeper than the surface level laughs, though, because I know that my relationship to Mia is precarious in some ways. I am not her parent. I will always come back, but possibly not as often as proximity allows right now. What if I get a job in another town, or another state? Things will change. Already I see her less than when I was her nanny.

The next Friday night I come over so that Carla and Lindsey can go out for dinner and a movie. When I open the door, Mia runs up and leaps into my arms. I might have been feeling a little down about giving up my Friday night to babysit, but now that seems like a shallow concern. I am with my girl tonight.

I heat up the leftovers Carla left for us, bring the plates of vegetarian polenta casserole to the table, steady Mia's hand as she pours her own glass of milk. We sit down and hold hands, the way she does every night with her parents. We each say something we are grateful for.

"I'm grateful for you," Mia grins. She always says this when I come over.

"I'm grateful for you, too."

She says the blessing Carla taught her, which she memorized. "Come Lord Jesus, our guest to be, and bless these gifts bestowed by thee. Amen."

After dinner, as a special treat, Carla had told her we could make popcorn and watch *The Wizard of Oz*. Mia helps me measure the corn kernels and pour them into a pot on the stove. She tries her best to be patient as we wait for them to pop.

"Shhh, listen!" she says, because I am talking too much. "I think they're starting to pop!"

When the sputtering and sizzling and popping slows I lift the lid, show her the fluffy white kernels, drizzle butter over it and shake on the salt. Mia carries the napkins and bowls out to the living room, and I put the movie in. As we settle into the couch, I marvel at how life can change, how this one small person has taught me how to live.

Mia taught me how to love. She taught me that I have more to offer the people around me than I ever could have seen in myself. She taught me this in part because her love for me has never depended on how smart or successful I am, but on the fact that I am there for her.

I didn't know. I just didn't know that I could love someone so much. I think that this is one of the best and most difficult things in my life, to have so much love, and to be searching for places to put it. It hurts to hold onto it. It is not meant to be all mine, it is meant to be given away.

As I edge closer to thirty, more and more of my friends are married. I get asked far too often if I want to get married, if I want to have children. People who know about my relationship with Mia think they know the answer. They seem to assume I want children, that I feel a certain emptiness because I have none of my own. When they actually ask me about it, though, more often than not my answer is, "I don't know."

Maybe. Maybe not. The question makes no sense to me in the abstract. Do I want to *be* married, as a state of being? Whatever. The question is unintelligible to me outside of the particulars of potential partners. Do you want to marry *this person?* No. Yes. That is a question I could answer.

Kids though—kids you never really get to choose, at least not in that way. You choose to have them. You choose not to have them. But you do not get to choose which ones you have, and if how they turn out is some unknown combination of nurture and nature, a lot of it is up to you.

I know that this is not what people are thinking of when they ask me these questions though.

My guess?

They're thinking, "Aren't you lonely?"

They're thinking, "Your life is incomplete."

They're thinking, "You'll regret your decisions someday."

I don't know. I only want to ask them, how could a life with so much love be lonely?

If you need to make sense of my relationship with Mia, you can call me her third mom, her nanny, her surrogate aunt, her friend.

She calls me her Meghan.

There is nothing lonely about that.

Bibliography

Breakfast at Tiffany's. Directed by Blake Edwards. 1961. Burbank, CA: Warner Home Video, 1999. DVD.

Kierkegaard, Søren. *Fear and Trembling; Repetition*. Translated by Howard V. and Edna H. Hong. Princeton, NJ: Princeton University Press, 1983.

———. *The Point of View*. Translated by Howard V. and Edna H. Hong. Princeton, NJ: Princeton University Press, 1998.

———. *Stages on Life's Way*. Translated by Howard V. and Edna H. Hong Princeton, NJ: Princeton University Press, 1988.

———. *Works of Love*. Translated by Howard V. and Edna H. Hong. Princeton, NJ: Princeton University Press, 1995.

Wolterstorff, Nicholas. *Lament for a Son*. Grand Rapids: William B. Eerdmans, 1987.